21 Deadly Myths of Parenting and 21 Creative Alternatives

21 Deadly Myths of PARENTING

And 21 Creative Alternatives

By Kenneth West, Ph.D.

Council Oak Books ■ Tulsa, Oklahoma

Council Oak Books
Tulsa, OK 74120

Printed in the United States of America
97 96 95 94 93 92 91 90   5 4 3 2 1

Library of Congress Catalog Card Number 90-81819
ISBN 0-933031-32-7

Design by Karen Slankard

To three women who have filled my life:

Mary Lewis West, my mother

Betty Leighton, my teacher

Patty Leight West, my wife

And to three men who did the same:

R. Frederick West, my father

Jim Leighton, my mentor

Pete Warren, my friend

CONTENTS

PREFACE

Myths are not falsehoods. They're simply beliefs people hold that are helpful to them during a particular era. For example, some cultures sacrificed virgins to earn the favor of the gods. Others held elaborate rain dances hoping to bring relief to the scorched earth. We smile when we review these ancient myths, but in their day they were deeply held convictions.

Because the raising of children has always been a primary task of adults, people in each age created myths to guide them. The ancient Greeks left handicapped children on a mountainside to die. The Turks offered my father-in-law their heart-felt sympathy after the birth of each of his six daughters. And we've only recently left a time when children were sent to factories and mines at an early age to work twelve to fourteen hours for pitiful wages. The times change. So do the myths that a culture supports and that support the culture.

Our parents struggled to discover better myths to raise us by, just as their parents before them did. My father, who was forced to take a bite of lye soap when he displeased his parents, abandoned that technique while raising us. Likewise, he left behind the "triple-spankings," which he loved to tell about. After he received a spanking in school, his mother spanked him when he returned home, and his father spanked him a third time when he returned from his ministerial duties.

Today, we inherit myths from the many generations before us. Although some remain helpful, many will not successfully prepare our children to live in the democracy and culture of the twenty-first century. As adults our children will live in a complex age where good communications and finely developed abilities will be required for men and women to succeed in careers, enrich marriages, provide quality homes for children and develop inward potentials. Already, most of us understand only too well the challenges that await our children.

Gone are the days of my mother's era, when her sister was forbidden to be a librarian because of the fear that books transmitted dreadful diseases. Gone are those days when women in the sixth grade were forced to choose between sewing and cooking classes, while men were left to pursue manly ventures. Gone are the days when divorce and stepfamilies were rare. Ours is a new age.

New healthy beliefs will propel our families into the future. This book examines 21 of the myths that may prove hazardous to your children. In their place, I discuss 21 beliefs that will help you to raise children who will be ready to succeed in a changing world. You may prefer all of the 21 new beliefs or you may wish to combine many of the newer ideas with a few of the old myths. What is important is that each parent works out the best available strategy for preparing the next generation to meet its challenges.

This book will allow you to view the crucial myths and beliefs of our time and to decide for yourself which ones are best for your family. Sure, times will change again. But until they do, shelve the lye soap and triple-spankings and use those techniques and skills that will help your children create fulfilling lives in the twenty-first century.

ACKNOWLEDGMENTS

So many wonderful families have passed my way. And it is to them that I owe my greatest appreciation. Seeing families struggle to grow in therapeutic situations and watching parents increase thier abilities to understand and work with their children through continuing education programs, inspired me to write this book.

Writing takes patience and time — not only from the writer, but also from family members. My wife Patty improved each chapter by adding her ideas and comments. More, she modeled the beliefs within this volume daily in her relationships with our three children: Patrick, Emily and Dustin. She is the spirit within these pages. A special thanks to each of our children for their patience in hearing about the book so often and their tolerance of being used frequently as examples — good and bad. I'm pleased that they have become among my best friends and supporters.

Without the enthusiasm and love with which my mother Mary Lewis West and my father the late R. Frederick West raised me and my siblings, I would never have entered the field of child development and family counseling. To them goes my eternal appreciation.

Betty Leighton edited each chapter of this book and provided constant encouragement for me. I've never known a more learned person or a better friend.

A special thanks to Betty Shelton who typed the original drafts of the book. Also, a deeply-felt thanks to Ed Polloway, Pete Warren and Dave Smith at Lynchburg College for their strong support and constant friendship through the years. Lynchburg College provided funds that supported my work on the manuscript, and I greatly appreciate the College's help.

Past teachers always deserve special recognition. The many fine professionals who are members of the North American Society of Adlerian Psychology have been outstanding teachers of parents for decades and have influenced my ideas.

Also, I would like to thank my editors Billy Cline and Cecil Mullan at the *News and Daily Advance* (Lynchburg, Virginia) who not only shared their enthusiasm over my column *Family Focus* but also shared their valuable ideas about the art of writing.

Sally Dennison and Michael Hightower at Council Oak Books deserve special praise for their dedication to make each manuscript unique and exciting. They've made me feel like a member of the Council Oak family.

Finally, I would like to thank the leaders and families that have worked together for these past fourteen years in our Parent Study Program, supported by Lynchburg College, Randolph-Macon Woman's College, and the Virginia Baptist Hospital. Particularly, I would like to thank Gretchen Morgan and Peggy Friend for their leadership. Without the families we have known, our lives would be less full.

MYTH 1

PARENTING SHOULD COME NATURALLY

You are the best parent your child will ever have. But how did you learn to parent? For most of us parenting becomes, in part, a demanding, often frustrating profession for which we receive no formal training. Almost two decades of school work included no courses in potty training toddlers or handling adolescent rebellion. And certainly, no one was prepared to live with a troublesome child or to handle the challenges commonly faced by single parents or stepparents.

Yet, suddenly there you stand with a two-year-old throwing a public temper tantrum amidst a crowd of critics who wait for your response. Your mind races. But your past A's in square root deduction offer no help. Your knowledge of Shakespeare's sonnets and your ability to type 70 words per minute fail to save you. None of your hours in class helps. So where do you turn?

Most turn to a set of myths imperfectly learned from their parents. When misbehavior occurred, perhaps it seemed that our parents yelled or spanked or did nothing. We usually imitate whatever they did. Or, in some cases, we do the opposite. While few parents feel confident that these techniques work well in our era, we often are tied to our models and myths of the past. Why? Because parenting does not come naturally.

In addition to our limited education, the times have changed. When childhood became more complicated, parenting became more complex.

The New World of Childhood

Captain Kangaroo lost his place long ago to mechanical heroes who rid the earth of menacing robots and computers gone astray. Action never stops. Electronic media brings the pain and violence of the world into our homes. At night, when I dare turn to the television news, terrorists seem to spring out of the set to blow up another part of the world. In the old days — according to the romantic production, *Oklahoma!* — couples would "sit alone and talk and watch a hawk makin' lazy circles in the sky." Now the hawk's circles are lost in jet streams, and family talk is buried beneath the sound of rock videos and blaring stereos.

Children encounter school pressures unknown in their parents' school days. Elementary school tests exist in such numbers that my children own more percentile rankings than cat-eye marbles. Homework pours in from kindergarten classes, and by the time a child reaches fourth grade, parents couldn't help with homework if they wanted to. Fifth-graders anticipate SATs and can recite various colleges' entrance requirements. It is as if years ago childhood was placed in a time capsule and launched somewhere into a galaxy far, far away from our universe.

Families changed along the way, too. Single parents who once dreamed of enjoying an enriching marriage and raising peaceful kids find themselves raising children alone in an atmosphere similar to that of the New York City subways. For single parents, life escalates to a frantic pace, one for which most are untrained. Escaping the parenting subway seems impossible. Any helpful hints from knowledgeable bystanders are received as a blessing.

Remarriage multiplies the number of stepfamilies in society. Parents of stepfamilies rarely served internships in blended homes. In stepfamilies, the rules for sanity change from day to day. Not receiving helpful instruction on how to coexist is like playing chess without a rule book. Sometimes just discovering how the pieces move proves helpful.

Dual-career parents swell in number. They select caregivers with the scrutiny their parents reserved for buying a first home. For many people, family support disappeared with increased mobility. Scattered families gather only for major occasions, and they often appear more unified than they really are. In fact, some parents call their babysitters to share the news of a child's first step before they notify their own brothers and sisters.

Added to the waves of adults entering the new, stressful world of parenting are those couples who traditionally require counsel. Poor modeling from their own parents leaves many new parents unprepared to pursue family life. Often, husbands and wives come from radically different home experiences. As a result, complicated relationships often evolve, for example, when one parent disciplines as an authoritarian and the other with permissiveness. Desperate for common ground, disharmonious couples flounder until help arrives or children leave home.

Despite dramatic changes and challenges within a complex world, many parents maintain: "We don't need advice. Parenting comes naturally." You know these parents. Most fathers who maintain that raising children is natural rarely participate in child care. Usually the mother carries the load. The father scurries away at the break of dawn, enjoying the safety of his workplace and returns late in the evening in time for supper.

Complicated relationships often evolve, for example, when one parent disciplines as an authoritarian and the other with permissiveness.

Families with omniscient dads occasionally wander into family counseling. One such father I named Dump Truck Charlie. Every Tuesday he would drop his family at my office door, order them inside, and wait in the parking lot until the kids were fixed. Because he insisted that discipline was his wife's problem, he avoided learning anything new. Dump Truck Charlie never learned to display his love or to discipline peacefully. His family lived limited lives because of the myth that father knows best.

From where do we receive advice on parenting? All of us seem related to an Aunt Bertha Perfect. Usually an Aunt Bertha raised six children, all poorly, but she becomes the family expert because of her years in service. After examining Aunt Bertha's children, you realize that not one of them developed an enviable personality. To Aunt Bertha results don't matter, but effort and sacrifice do. She donated her life to her kids and it appears they squandered it. She raised six children mistakenly six different times, yet she's proud of her consistency. Aunt Bertha never asked for advice, and obviously none was given.

Aunt Bertha donated her life to her kids and it appears they squandered it.

Marvin and Annie Archives know exactly how you should raise your children. For them life never changed. They raise children as their parents and their grandparents did. As you enter their home, you notice that small glass statues of birds and other breakable relics from frontier days are at the grasping level of their children. Something seems wrong.

The children join you in the living room and sit quietly with hands folded in their laps. With eyes like opossum's, they are apparently listening to every adult word, smiling at appropriate times. The adult conversations include discussions of traditions and long-lost cousins.

After what seems to have been hours spent honoring the past, you begin to wonder why this family changed to indoor plumbing. Soon, your uneasy feeling about the kids is understood. Even Aunt Bertha's kids seem more dynamic. The Archives raise children who exhibit no passion and little energy. No advice for raising children proved necessary because this home prohibits childhood.

NEW AND IMPROVED BELIEF 1
PARENT EDUCATION
HELPS EVERYONE

Although all parents can benefit from quality parent education, traditionally only the most skillful parents pursue such opportunities. As in other areas of life, the rich psychologically grow richer. As a naive young professor my sole question after offering free classes for parents was: Where are the parents who need education? Parenting programs fill with talented adults hungry for new ideas and techniques.

Occasionally, programs provide parents who are low in skills with opportunities to study. Parents who have been deprived of adequate parental models improve quickly by learning basic principles of communication and discipline. A grant allowed our local court system to mandate classes for parents of first-time offenders. One such mother, Mary Sadling, had no control in her home. Although she was a caring mother, the word "No" never sprang from her lips. She developed into a "Try-To Parent."

Whenever her adolescents issued even the most absurd request, she responded: "Try to be back home early." "Try to stay away from Timothy Ward." "Try not to go to the Do Drop Inn." Obviously, her children ignored her "try to" pleas and followed their own desires. Their paths led to delinquency.

What tremendous improvement Mary Sadling and her family experienced when she learned to establish "bottom lines" and to act. Parents with few skills enjoy

> Parents who have been deprived of adequate parental models improve quickly by learning basic principles of communication and discipline.

gigantic strides by adding basic parenting skills in communications and in the use of consequences.

Some parents must learn to become less able. Perfectionists suffer from a serious parenting disability which spreads tension like chicken pox. Requirements for perfection in behavior, achievement, social skills and happiness imprison children within a parent's own insecurities.

Anne Johnson maintained straight A's through college. With the birth of her first child, she gave up her interests to devote full attention to raising a proper child. Accustomed to pleasing faculty members with her work, she was unsure how to parent for applause. The solution seemed simple: Perfect children earn rave reviews from everyone.

But to raise a prodigy, she must share his perfection. To do this, Anne began to grade herself. Her internal gradebook recorded only A's and F's. One public temper tantrum by her two-year-old brought Anne the grade of F. Any child advancing faster than hers threw Anne into depressions of inadequacy. She just couldn't master perfection. Her child appeared to be untrainable, not to mention unappreciative of her sacrifices. When Anne gained some knowledge of child development, she made the discovery that the difficulty was in her grading system rather than in her child. Perfectionism prevents the healthy growth of children, because misbehavior is a normal part of childhood.

Not infrequently, advice for parents unites bickering couples. Jack and Mary Holden come from childhood homes dominated by opposite myths. The sword and paddle ruled Jack's home, while Mary's parents disciplined by hugging. After the birth of the Holdens' first child, confusion played the lead role in their family. Neither Jack nor Mary liked or respected their spouse's favorite myths. A marital rift began to widen when their child's misbehavior increased as he grew older. By studying the art of parenting, the couple found a common ground that became the foundation for family peace.

Parent education helps everyone. Whether parents are competent or underskilled, they will benefit by adding new techniques and knowledge.

All couples, but particularly those who face challenging family situations, such as stepfamilies who must blend several traditions of parenting, will feel comfort in discovering a common ground for raising children. As a result, their children will prosper.

NEW PITFALL 1
EXPERTS ALWAYS KNOW BEST

You are the best parents your child will ever have. You know your children, yourself and your family better than any authority can. Authorities often offer good advice, but sometimes your family and the advice don't mix. No single method for raising children fits all families.

Authorities rarely understand the unique traits of a parent or the family's personality as a whole. For example, some families exhibit a sense of humor that allows them to handle difficulties in a relaxed manner. Humor reduces confrontation and tolerates imperfection. But not all families enjoy humor as part of the family personality; therefore, specialists overlook such virtues.

Other parents handle challenges with creativity and flexibility. Still others possess a mother lode of common sense. None of these attributes seems contagious. In fact, most adults observe creative or sensible parents and exclaim, "Why didn't I think of that?" Many parents imitate but rarely generate common sense. General advice should never be substituted for natural parenting strengths.

No single method for raising children fits all families.

19

Your family's uniqueness deserves preservation.

Parents are mistaken to place too much credence in an authority's opinion. Margaret Hopkins possessed a gift for love and fair play. She taught her child never to bite, pinch or hit. Consequences were used whenever offenses occurred. Margaret enrolled her child in a preschool where the "authority" tried to teach children to protect their individual space. The class rule instructed children to strike back when struck: "An eye for an eye, and a tooth for a tooth." Instead of following her own inclinations, the parent adopted the "expert's" philosophy. Soon her children became neighborhood outcasts. No parent would allow a child to play with a youngster who was encouraged to retaliate in barbaric ways.

Parenting experts offer good advice, but their beliefs remain their myths until they fit your world. If they fit, then utilize the ideas and enjoy the results. But always be skeptical. Your family's uniqueness deserves preservation. Remember: Be patient with parenting experts. Recall how little experience they have had with your family.

MYTH 2

GOOD CHILDREN NEVER MISBEHAVE

Like cockroaches, the myth of perfect children prospers through time despite all attempts at extermination. No myth creates more parental feelings of guilt and inadequacy than this misguided doctrine that good children never misbehave. The greatest agents for the myth's perpetuation appear to be childless relatives, forgetful grandparents and child-raising experts from out of town.

Good children misbehave. They sporadically violate home rules and particularly enjoy the practice of frustrating parents who hold unrealistic expectations. However, many annoying misbehaviors contribute positively to the creation of an autonomous, free-thinking individual. Not all misbehaviors enjoy redeeming side-effects, but all healthy children misbehave occasionally.

Many adults observe, "I don't recall that we misbehaved as frequently as this generation does." They misbehaved and fail to remember. Why? I discovered the answer: Preparenting Amnesia. Therapists for decades argued about why adults remember so few of the thousands of events in childhood. If adults did remember the difficulty they created for their parents, I suspect most would remain childless. Thus, Preparenting Amnesia's adaptive quality allows the species to perpetuate. Unfortunately, a side-effect of the amnesia allows the pesky myth of perfection to infest new generations. Although most parents occasionally admit feeling overwhelmed by the demands of disciplining children, the majority survive. Making realistic parental adjustments to the challenges presented by their children allows parents to enjoy their children, and this helps to balance frustration and pleasure. Nevertheless, not all adults discover happiness in parenthood. Some only survive.

Few psychologists admit what most privately discuss: Not all adults should raise children. The myth of child perfection lures many, who might lead happier childless lives, to bear children. Those infected by the perfection myth expect to raise miniature adults who adapt to parental schedules. Those suffering from PMAS (Parenting Miniature Adults Syndrome) expect perfect obedience and dislike the challenges to their daily lives that children bring. These parents wish to love without inconvenience.

Those addicted to the perfect behavior myth often pursue unrealistic goals. For example, the pursuit of perfect behavior brings many to parenting class with the hope of immediately transforming a child into a responsible adult. Parents seeking perfection remind me of the old story of the misguided medical school applicant who hoped entry to medical school would insure immunity from physical disease. Quality medical care, like discipline, may reduce the frequency of difficulties, but will not eliminate the challenges.

The Slovicks spent ten weeks in a parenting course. Never were they happy. No matter what techniques we studied, they reported with shock the next week, "But our children still misbehave." Never did it dawn on the Slovicks that discipline never totally eliminates misbehavior. Years after the Slovicks' angry departure, I occasionally encounter Mrs. Slovick who asks, predictably: "Do you still believe in the same techniques now that your three children are older? My response is, "Yes, and I still believe children must occasionally misbehave. . . ." She frowns, then stalks off toward a more intelligent conversationalist.

Some adults tolerate limited misbehavior but are deeply disturbed because the birth of a child changes their adult lifestyle. They wish to love without sacrifice. While well-equipped for Pet Parenting, these adults become unhappy with the changes that parenting children inevitably brings to their personal routines.

The Jenkins entered their fifteenth year of marriage before their first baby arrived. Immediately the baby interfered with their carefully wrought life patterns. Still, the new parents longed to join their friends on evenings and weekends, travel through Europe in the summer and lead a generally unrestricted life. Growing anger toward their child's intrusions brought the Jenkins to counseling. Neither the parents nor the child displayed true misbehaviors. Miscast together, they were ill-suited for a family performance. The Jenkins preferred a warm, loving addition to the family who would remain faithful during long and frequent absences. As Pet Parents, the Jenkins would have excelled.

Single parents and stepparents often face the additional challenge of not knowing whether their children's disturbing behavior is "normal" or is a result of their family's unique pressures. Many misbehaviors of a child represent his or her way of responding to grief, anger, anxiety or powerlessness. Although parents must respond to these misbehaviors, the acts may be the only methods that their children know which express their feelings. It requires time for young people to learn to share their feelings maturely. To expect perfection from children who

Many misbehaviors of a child represent his or her way of responding to grief, anger, anxiety or powerlessness.

One of the marvels of education remains that some students manage to memorize thousands of facts about children but fail to understand childhood.

already feel stress in life simply adds to the pressures that they experience.

Some adults never manage to overcome the myth of perfect behavior despite earning impressive credentials. A few of these chronic sufferers collect graduate degrees and choose professions working with children. One of the marvels of education remains that some students manage to memorize thousands of facts about children but fail to understand childhood. Despite years of study many exhibit Terminal Insight Deprivation.

Recently a graduate of my course, which explores the predictable misbehaviors of childhood, cornered me at a picnic and warned, "I'll be watching to see if your kids misbehave." My youngest cried when he was not allowed a second balloon. The graduate student shook his head in horror. His belief in perfect behavior proved resistant to education. He earned an A in class, but an F in reality.

On the other hand, many persons with little formal education understand children. They possess a brilliance for living. All of us know such natural students. One local convenience-store clerk is the mother of six children and the grandmother of three. She handles every child who enters the store with a sophisticated expertise I often envy. Although her formal education was brief, she lives her life free of the chains of parenting's most debilitating myth: Good children never misbehave.

**NEW AND IMPROVED BELIEF 2
GOOD CHILDREN
MUST MISBEHAVE**

Children exhibit an unbridled spirit at birth. Their behavior and thinking express a passion and uniqueness not yet eroded by socialization.

But children inherit no innate sense of identity. Children discover themselves by testing limits and experimenting with behaviors that separate them from their parents. These behaviors prove frustrating to many parents. When children cross boundaries and defy parents, adults consider such acts to be useless misbehavior. But many misbehaviors serve as necessary experiments in the building of identity. Guidelines, constructive discipline and encouragement reduce these misbehaviors and encourage positive identities. However, misbehavior must continue if a child is to achieve independence and identity.

Arnold Gesell, founder of the Gesell Institute of Child Development, beautifully describes a child's innate push to create identity. He maintains that a child alternates every few months between conformity and rebellion. When they feel courageous, children push against life's walls, testing both their own and their parents' limits. Then, like tired warriors they retreat to the secure home of conformity until the tide of energy arises for another assault on life. Such behaviors, like natural ocean tides, are part of life. And, as with tides, parents will fail to subdue a child's natural cycle without creating more complicated problems.

In addition to the natural drives that a child exhibits when creating identity, there exist well-known watermarks in childhood when positive growth creates predictable challenges for parents.

At about the age of eight months, stranger anxiety occurs. Until then youngest grandchildren enjoy a favored position. Suddenly, the grandparents' joy at seeing their

> **When they feel courageous, children push against life's walls, testing both their own and their parents' limits.**

grandchild is spoiled by a barrage of tears. Although stranger anxiety deserves a celebration of the child's new ability to distinguish primary caretakers, it often sets in motion the Family Disinheritance Process.

Another well known occasion for misbehavior occurs around the second year. The "terrible twos" serve as a preview of adolescence and, for some, become proof that the Creator has a wry sense of humor. Trying to separate himself from parents, a two-year-old asserts identity in an unmistakable fashion. The word "no" becomes a password to autonomy. Variations of the declaration, "No," abound. My favorite is: "Don't even look at me!" The most often heard may be: "I do it myself!"

Although two-year-olds defy authority at every turn, their misbehaviors symbolize a healthy growth toward independence. Well-considered responses to rebellion are necessary, but overreaction can squash newly born identities.

Mary and James Sprouse fought the "terrible twos." They refused to "be pushed around by their child." Their misguided philosophy suggested that any form of "no" constituted disrespectful rebellion and required stiff resistance.

The opportunity to fight with their two-year-old came daily. Spankings and screaming followed each movement toward childhood autonomy. Beaten down by their child, the Sprouses limped into therapy, the veterans of many a lost power struggle. Although their family had become embroiled in friction and unhappiness, the Sprouses eventually broke free of the myth that good children never misbehave.

A broken spirit is a severe price to pay for parental needs.

Sometimes, parents at war with children can destroy a child's spirit. Sadly, such adults believe that some parental or moral victory is won when they have overwhelmed a child. The victims of overzealous and misguided parents are the Shark-Eyed Children of our culture. Shark-Eyed Children surrender their spirit, in order to avoid repeated psychological or physical abuse. A broken spirit is a severe price to pay for parental needs.

If Mom and Dad form the seawall for a two-year-old's wrath, the world provides the fortress for a four-year-old's attacks. Boundaries are examined, crossed and pushed out. Children this age are like gas seeking containment. Again, what many consider misbehavior often represents a searching for possibilities in life.

In our latest family fishing fiasco, I played everything by the book. All three of my children listened to an exquisite lecture concerning the do's and don'ts of fishing. A demonstration on how to throw a line on a cane pole followed. When I finished, chaos set in.

Only the fish were safe. Everyone else cringed with fright. Flying hooks snagged tree limbs, stumps, discarded junk and low-flying birds. After two hours, exhaustion overtook the adults. My patience, and the trip, ended when our four-year-old tossed the worms in the lake to watch them swim. Misbehavior? Yes and no. The death of the worms ended a fishing trip, yet it satisfied the questions of a young explorer.

Predictable challenges continue through adolescence. Teens experience the most publicized push to create identity and to separate themselves from their parents. Identity comes slowly in our complicated society. Teens determine their own beliefs within a society of mixed messages.

Adults champion opposing stances on moral and social issues such as sex, religion, and war. National and state governments send confusing signals concerning when adulthood arrives. For example, a teen can die for his country at eighteen, but in most states cannot buy alcoholic beverages until three years later. Yet at sixteen he receives the keys to our greatest killer: the car. All of this confusion occurs while new hormones ricochet through the body.

Teens determine their own beliefs within a society of mixed messages. All of this confusion occurs while new hormones ricochet through the body.

While struggling toward identity, teens separate themselves from parents to create a personal autonomy that will enable them to venture alone into the world. This separation may require many small storms and an occasional earthquake. Sometimes adolescents seem to ask parents about their beliefs so they can then tell them how they failed. The price of growth is conflict. No strategies prevent teens from challenging authority and rules. These misbehaviors remain necessary for the creation of their independence.

Sometimes humor becomes a parent's most useful survival weapon. The 16-year-old son of a close friend of mine lambasted him for not giving more money to the teenager's favorite charity. The son characterized the father as a self-centered skinflint. Defensively, the father responded, "And how much have you donated?" Angrily the son retorted: "Nothing, but that's not a fair question. You know I am saving my money to buy a stereo."

During each year, misbehaviors occur which represent a positive striving for autonomy and personal growth. Supporting a myth that maintains that good children never misbehave will insure years of parental guilt and frustration. Good children *must* misbehave and leave perfection for us!

NEW PITFALL 2
"IT'S JUST A STAGE"

Some misbehavior is obnoxious and useless. Such misbehaviors benefit no one and add nothing to the virtues of human growth. Positive discipline must be used. Other misbehaviors represent a child's drive for growth but also require discipline. Some parents use a little knowledge to the disadvantage of society. Such parents watch their child's hideous behavior, then look into the faces of terrified onlookers and remark, "Oh, it's just a stage." We all know this comment means that the parent plans to do nothing that will save us from the hooligan.

At a birthday party, three-year-old Timothy Wilkins popped balloons and tore down decorations. He shoved other kids and drowned out all conversation with his ear-shattering screams. But Mrs. Wilkins looked on with admiration. At one point she turned to me and said, "Aren't three-year-olds just the cutest things?" Before I could be honest and reply, "Some are, but yours is totally out of control," Timothy knocked his mother's ice cream on to her lap. No matter how productive or useless the misbehavior, parents must respond.

MYTH 3

**GOOD PARENTS
SHOULD NEVER
LOSE THEIR TEMPER**

Myths that stifle the freedom of emotional expression flourish in our society. By accepting myths, such as, "good parents should never lose their temper," adults develop emotional handicaps that hinder communications and narrow relationships. Worse still, children who model parental weaknesses may continue these disabilities for another generation. Some myths attack people's comfort in expressing any level of anger, while others discourage the sharing of love or vulnerability.

Myths that steal emotions create awkward humans who are out of step with their natural feelings. One parenting book, for example, describes the following misbehavior, then suggests an amusing parental response. The case reads something like this: "Mr. Jones entered his workshop. There he found Tommy painting the last of Mr. Jones's new worktools. The tools still dripped with ugly red paint. Mr. Jones looked at his newly painted tools, then at Tommy and said, 'I see you painted my tools. We have a problem here. What do you think we should do

**Myths that
steal emotions
create awkward
humans who
are out of
step with their
natural feelings.**

about it?'" This example propagates the restrictive myth that good parents should never lose their temper.

Unless Mr. Jones's goals in life include becoming a computer, his response seems unrealistic and, at best, made for situation comedy. Well-intended advice from experts often reinforces myths that emotionally debilitate parents and leave them feeling guilty and frustrated.

Parents Should Not Show Anger

Somewhere, anger picked up a bad reputation in our society. Despite the fact that everyone experiences anger and that anger frequently encourages appropriate responses to complex situations, some consider anger to be an unnecessary, primitive emotion. Try to imagine a parent who disdains anger becoming involved in a crisis situation where a stranger approaches the Angerless Parent's child and beats the child furiously. Would the emotionless parent respond: "Excuse me, Sir. It appears you are beating my child. I have a problem with that. Please stop striking him or I must inform the proper authorities."

Interestingly enough, a few religious educators aggressively teach that feeling anger is sinful. Some teach that in every situation, good people must "turn the other cheek." How difficult it must be for them to rationalize the story of Jesus driving the moneychangers from the temple!

In some situations, adults feel that it's "not their right" to express anger, even when provoked. Particulary susceptible to such mistaken thinking are single parents and stepparents. Somehow they've grown to believe that the children in the family have the right to free emotional expression, but the adults do not.

Parental anger is a human emotion that is, at times, a natural reaction to a child's behavior. Anger should not

> **Somewhere, anger picked up a bad reputation in our society.**

The Great Emotional Dam Model fits many who oppose the expression of any anger.

be directed toward the child as a person but toward the misbehavior which elicited the anger. True, many hostile adults misuse anger. Their responses attack the child rather than the misbehavior. Hostility violates a child and serves no fruitful purpose. Unfortunately, hostility and other misuses of anger ruin anger's reputation. All humans must cope with anger. Parents, children's major models, provide a variety of interesting methods for handling anger.

The Great Emotional Dam Model fits many who oppose the expression of any anger. These parents never voice anger, blocking its natural flow with a wall of calm. As time passes, they apparently lose access to hard emotions such as anger. Children of these parents assume that good people never express emotion. Yet these children do experience anger and if they remain unable to hide the prohibited feeling from others, anxiety and guilt soon follow.

Once I encountered Mrs. Smythe, a woman in her mid-forties, whose husband deserted her and their three adolescents. Soon afterward, the daughter became incorrigible, staying out later and later at night, and the son became his mother's personal critic, often abusing her in public. Yet in our counseling sessions, Mrs. Smythe sat passively in her chair without the slightest display of emotion and placidly took her children's punches without response. Any discussion of anger triggered her tiresome response, "It isn't nice to be angry." By damming up anger, Mrs. Smythe became powerless, unable to summon the emotion needed to fight for her rights. Mrs. Smythe's avoidance of anger left her defenseless.

A similar approach attempts to dam anger but eventually explodes with volcanic fury. This Mt. St. Parent Approach creates difficulties for children. Because the release of anger appears unpredictable, children cannot anticipate an oncoming eruption. Also, eruption survivors remain unsure of what brought about the explosion.

Therefore, anxious children baby their volcanic parents, hoping not to overexcite them. Children must tread softly around the base of an unstable and frightening force. Ironically, Mt. St. Parents fight the natural release of anger until the unleashed emotion boils into an uncontrolled outburst.

Many parents openly display natural anger, although they feel their expressions of anger are wrong. As a consequence they feel guilt. This Parental Guiltfill Condition assumes that anger harms the child in an irreversible way. Even those parents who learn as adults that anger is an appropriate feeling may find that intellectual discoveries rarely erase childhood impressions. These adults face an interesting dilemma. As that skilled myth-fighter Albert Ellis, founder of Rational Emotive Therapy, explains, the parent experiences double guilt: guilt over expressing anger, then guilt over feeling guilty about displaying anger.

Children's behaviors occasionally arouse parental feelings of anger that are natural and sometimes helpful. For example, a young child who dresses slowly needs to know that this misbehavior is not the equivalent of running into the middle of a busy street. Anger, expressed over serious misbehaviors, makes this point. Similarly, a parent whose adolescent stays out until 4:00 a.m. often lets the child know in a memorable fashion that such misbehaviors are not allowable. Consequences alone do not always make this point. Anger rarely solves problems, but it allows those involved to understand the severity of certain situations.

Anger sometimes occurs naturally but becomes counterproductive. Nevertheless, some spontaneous eruptions appear innocent and understandable. For example, my daughter unleashes a verbal explosion that combines a cloud-dispersing yell with a life-threatening whine. On the East Coast, this outburst is known as The Emily Shriek. Neighborhood children coach her in the shriek's

> **Many parents openly display natural anger, although they feel their expressions of anger are wrong. As a consequence they feel guilt.**

most effective use. I can imagine their instructions: "OK, let's try this again from the top. Your dad comes home from work exhausted and frustrated. He's trying to pull his life together with a moment of peace. You and your brothers run into the room. Your brother looks at you funny and that's your cue to UNLOAD right into your old man's ear: The Emily Shriek."

Maybe you know an Emily Shriek. Ours has spent time in her room, been talked to reasonably, and suffered consequences. But The Shriek resists extinction — and so does the resultant parental anger.

Occasionally, parents who risk sharing emotions such as anger overreact. Such displays of anger may be unfortunate, but they need not be detrimental. As cognitive theorists might point out: "What's the big deal? So you lost your temper."

After such episodes, avoid another sick myth (Love means never having to say you are sorry) and apologize to your child. Children love to hear parents admit, "I goofed." Explain why your temper escaped its usual boundaries. A parent showing courage in admitting an error becomes a positive model for a child. Youngsters too will make mistakes with emotions. In observing a parent's humanness and ability to handle errors, children experience their own emotions and shortcomings with less guilt and anxiety.

> **Anger rarely solves problems, but it allows those involved to understand the severity of certain situations.**

Real Men Don't Say, "I Love You."

Many adults in our society impersonate a Cowardly Lion or Lioness. But instead of traveling to Oz in search of the courage to express tenderness, they celebrate a myth implying that the sharing of intimate feelings displays weakness. In the parental lions' attempts not to appear weak, they lack the courage to share life's most celebrated emotion. Ironically, cowardice prevents most parental lions from securing courage.

Children need the assurance that they are loved. With divorce and remarriage rates soaring, and with schedules overflowing, children profit by knowing that, despite major life changes and distractions, they are loved.

Most parents recognize a child's need to experience love, but many are unable to share love directly. Instead they communicate tender feelings through another source. One such common source Salvador Minuchin, founder of Structural Family Therapy, labels, "Switchboard Moms." These moms relay tender messages from father to child. Too often a child hears mother report: "Your dad really does love you and he is so proud of you. He just has a hard time telling you that."

Children of Switchboard Moms may spend a lifetime trying to gain direct approval and expressions of love from their father, but usually these efforts fail. The Switchboard Mom protects the father from his weakness and enjoys too much power over family communications to allow change. Children become victims of a family emotional disability.

Mothers and children may also indirectly relay feelings of tenderness. And in some extreme cases entire families exist without sharing intimacy, even in indirect ways.

On the other hand, some adults spout "I love you" so frequently that no emotion arrives with the message. At a picnic I recently heard a mother profess, "I love you," to her child six times in a single hour. On cue the child responded with the same words but without loving emotions. The scene resembles those moments before a meal when small children race through a required blessing without giving the words any meaning. Too often said, "I love you" becomes a greeting, a kind of simple salutation that fails to assure a child of the sentiment's depth.

Some say "I love you" with emotion but encounter difficulty acting in a loving way. For example, at a school lunch one emotional parent greeted her daughter with a warm hug, kiss and statement of love. But as soon as the meal began the mother berated her, at one point slapping her for dropping food. If parental misbehavior like this represents love to the child, woe to the next generation of children!

Many loving parents express their love in symbolic ways that children cannot understand. Virginia Satir, the famous family therapist, often asked parents, "What do you do to show your child love?" Many replied: "I work ten hours every day and provide for the family. In fact, we own a second home at the beach. My kids have things I never dreamed of owning."

Often children of hard workers feel unloved. Why? Because children prefer parents to benefactors. Love requires time and patience. Nevertheless, some parents avoid intimacy, choosing to display love from a safe distance.

Physical expressions of love enrich many parent-child relationships.

Physical expressions of love enrich many parent-child relationships. How fortunate are children whose parents hug and kiss them regularly. Physical contact assures children of love, while well-filled cupboards, second homes and cars only relay concern.

Lions without courage provide well, and they love children. But their distant expression of love often misses the mark. Come close. Take time to hug your child and talk directly of love. Every lion needs the courage to express love.

Parents Should Not Share Vulnerability

America champions strength. Our movies unfurl and idolize rock-hard humans, from magnum-carrying detectives to super human soldiers to judo masters cleaning the streets of unruly vermin. Human vulnerability appears only in scripts for comedy and satire. Many parents promote the myth of invulnerability by hiding fragile feelings from children.

Carefully hiding any feelings of hurt, fear, disappointment or anxiety, this Parental Fortress Model prepares children for life in cinema but not for life in this world. Putting a strong foot forward, parents hold back tears at funerals, show a stiff upper lip following the loss of jobs or dreams, and approach triple-bypass surgery without fear or anxiety. Surrounded by strength, children at times feel inadequate when experiencing their own grief, hurt, and disappointment; others assume that after reaching adulthood, their feelings of vulnerability disappear. Far from disappearing, fragile feelings become imprisoned within the adult fortress.

Parents often mask vulnerable feelings by converting them to hard feelings. For example, a Super Mom's family came to me for counseling because of the mother's anger toward uncooperative family members. Although Mr. Gentry urged his wife's reentry into the job world, he assumed no additional responsibility in the home. The mother fixed breakfast, drove the children to school, worked all day, then came home to cook dinner, wash clothes and dishes, and help the children to bed. In return her family incessantly complained that Mom was too busy for their usual enjoyable times together. But no one offered to help. Overwhelmed, Mrs. Gentry responded with anger.

She felt hurt by her family's lack of support and cooperation. She felt used and unloved.

Mrs. Gentry's anger hid feelings she feared: She felt hurt by her family's lack of support and cooperation. She felt used and unloved. Because her hurt feelings seemed a weakness, Mrs. Gentry hid them from her family and from herself by unleashing tirades of anger toward her family. But because anger was not the feeling central to the problem, the family made no progress. When Mrs. Gentry lowered the drawbridge to share her feelings of hurt and disappointment, the family quickly rallied to her support.

Parents mistakenly believe that children will not respond well to feelings of weakness. But children by nature experience smallness and weakness; therefore, they identify with similar parental experiences and enjoy opportunities to help adults.

Other vulnerable feelings (such as fear) challenge parental openness. For a child to ride a bicycle through busy streets or for a teenager to stay out late at night frightens parents. But adults may be uncomfortable sharing their fears. Instead, easier emotions to express such as anger or frustration may accompany conversations with children. "No!" Mom yells with anger, "You can't ride your bicycle to town; you are not old enough." Or, "No!" says a dad impatiently, "I told you a million times you cannot stay out past midnight as long as you live in this house." How different this scenario might be if parents would share their true feelings: "It scares me when you ride your bicycle near traffic. That's why I cannot let you go." Or: "I become frightened when you are out late. When I am frightened I imagine all kinds of terrible catastrophes, then I can't sleep. I am awake until I know you are safe in our house."

Some parental myths steal our humanity. Those myths that limit our expression of one or more emotions reduce our ability to communicate effectively and to share the richness and variety of responses experienced in living. "Good parents never lose their temper." Humbug!

NEW AND IMPROVED BELIEF 3
SHARE YOUR FEELINGS

Developing emotional potential equals in importance the development of academic possiblities. In fact, as a nation with an exploding adolescent suicide rate, where mental illness and life complications abound, we appear to be more dedicated to developing human thinking than human feeling. Although intellectual accomplishment may promote professional success, emotional growth provides the basics for rich personal relationships. Homes become the great emotional hatcheries of our nation. Sometimes an adult's own emotional upbringing has left much to be desired.

Adults learned most of their emotions from their parents. Most parents model, expect, and reward, healthy emotional responses to a variety of life situations. But all parents have limitations that may include poorly developed emotions in certain areas. Unfortunately these limitations may be passed on to another generation unless parents expand their emotional capabilities.

To develop emotional expressiveness more fully, parents first should examine their own ability to express feelings of love, anger or vulnerability. Which feelings find easy expression? Which are missing, or difficult to share? What myths did your parents teach through their expressions of emotions? Do you wish to accept these myths and pass them to your children? If not, then break out of the prison of past modeling.

After identifying and disowning useless emotional myths, slowly allow those once-prohibited feelings to surface. Share these feelings with a trusted friend, your spouse, or a counselor. One standard communication exercise which often helps, suggests beginning communications with the words, "I feel. . . " Then identify your feelings. Next, be specific about the circumstances leading to these feelings. The standard formula runs: "I feel X in situation Y when you do Z." For example, "I feel frightened when we are outdoors and you sneak up on the roof."

Identify and practice using emotion-filled words that

> **We appear to be more dedicated to developing human thinking than human feeling.**

are tough for you to say. Practice leads to easier emotional expression. While experimenting with expressing emotions, it helps to act as if difficult expressions come easily. Soon they will.

Children seem particularly receptive to fielding emotions of adults. Young children understand and express a wide range of feelings. Until they accept limiting myths, young people have no "hang-ups" about emotions. Ironically, children can nurture parents' budding feelings until the parents cure themselves of emotional disabilities. SHARE YOUR FEELINGS.

**NEW PITFALL 3
"MY CHILDREN CAN HANDLE
ALL OF MY FEELINGS"**

Sharing feelings with children requires some restraint. Children cannot understand the sources of all adult feelings, nor do they benefit from hearing others. Sometimes parents err and go too far. That's O.K., but a steady diet of unhelpful feelings should be avoided.

If nothing positive can emerge from sharing hard feelings with a child, then refrain from sharing those feelings. For example, a child's performance or behavior may disappoint you, even when the child does his best. Sharing your disappointment may discourage a child at the very time encouragement is needed. For example, to say, "I am so disappointed in your SAT scores!" probably is not helpful to a child who shares the same disappointment.

Also, anger occasionally becomes too intense and turns to hostility, which children never need. In one family an angry mother yelled at her children, who were five and seven years old: "I wish I could give you two to an orphanage. I can't stand either of you any more." She apparently said this often and expected her children to understand that these were only momentary feelings. Of course, they could not. Never use more force than is necessary to make important points.

Although children enjoy wide access to feelings, they cannot understand life events that create intense adult feelings. For example, even most adults fail to completely understand personal feelings surrounding divorce. Therefore, to expect a child to shoulder these complex feelings is unreasonable. Likewise, existential struggles, such as fear of death, hardly seem appropriate for children. These deep feelings need sharing, but other adults provide a more appropriate forum.

Phobias passed from parents to children become albatrosses for the new generation. Parents with unreasonable fears of dogs, snakes, spiders, airplanes or other commonplace objects and/or events need to avoid passing these fears to children. Avoid situations where children will observe irrational or inappropriate feelings. In most cases allow a spouse or another adult to model more appropriate emotions in threatening situations.

Many adult emotions are none of a child's business. For example, arguments and intense feelings arising between spouses should remain in the marital domain. Feelings such as jealousy or sexual frustrations obviously should not be shown or expressed before children. In addition, sharing hard feelings toward grandparents or other relatives whom the child frequently sees should be avoided. Yes, such feelings are important, but they are none of a child's business.

Share your feelings? Yes! But remember some feelings are inappropriate for sharing with children. Instead, express such feelings openly with other responsible adults. Remember a child's limitations and don't fall into emotional pitfalls.

Some feelings are inappropriate for sharing with children.

MYTH 4

"MRS. JONES, YOUR CHILDREN ARE SO MUCH ALIKE"

"You won't believe how different my children are!" Yes, I will. Unfortunately, parental folklore mistakenly suggests that children in the same family should share similar personalities. No myth finds less support. In fact, children in one family usually build opposite personalities. Children may share family values, but they rarely share personality traits.

The "All Alike" myth saddles parents with unrealistic responsibility. While parental involvement contributes significantly to the well-being and security of a child, ordinal position more directly influences a child's growing personality traits. Nevertheless, parents often anguish over children's individual differences. Their perplexity surfaces in comments such as: "What happened to my Tommy? I raised him just like the others." Or, "Parents should throw away the first child and start over with the second."

If a child's characteristics and life choices are radically different from parental dreams, disappointed parents formulate guilt-ridden questions of the heart, such as,

---

Unfortunately, parental folklore mistakenly suggests that children in the same family should share similar personalities. No myth finds less support.

"Where did I go wrong as a parent?" One graduate student grappled with her failure in raising the second of her three children. Mrs. Richards dreamed that all of her children would attend college, establish respectable careers and raise wholesome families. Her first child, Mary, earned straight A's and attended an Ivy League school. After graduation she married and became a successful computer scientist.

The third child, Samuel, also did well academically, and earned a full academic scholarship to attend a prestigious state university. Eventually he graduated from law school. Although he delayed marriage, Mrs. Richards felt confident that marriage would eventually occur. But the middle child, Sally, never attended college. Instead, she dropped out of mainline society to write poetry. None of her poetry reached print. Although Sally made many friends, she remained single, much to her mother's dismay. At age thirty Sally supported herself with odd jobs which enabled her to pursue her artistic interests. Although admitting that the daughter enjoyed apparent happiness, Mrs. Richards still felt she had failed as a mother: "Why couldn't she be like my other two? I know I failed her, but I don't know how." Questions of the heart plague parents. How can a child differ so much from her parents' dreams?

In another instance, a father silently questioned his son's disdain for "traditional" male interests. John Hershey's three sons shared their dad's tall, strong frame. As a former minor league baseball player, Mr. Hershey almost made it to the big leagues. Driven by the belief that his parents' lack of early involvement prevented his total success, John pushed all three of his own sons toward sports.

One child, Cal, prospered in baseball. Although not a professional prospect, this son earned his father's favor. The second son, Sam, became an outstanding high school football player, and also enjoyed his dad's approval. But

> Sometimes a child strays so far from family dreams that parents wonder if the child belongs in another galaxy, or whether a switch took place in the delivery room.

the third son, Mark, never displayed any interest in sports. He refused to participate and never cultivated basic athletic skills. Despite the fact that Mark excelled in school and became a successful teacher, Mr. Hershey always believed that his modeling failed. The sons' differences frightened the father. Surely, he thought, something went wrong with Mark. "Could it be my fault?" Mr. Hershey pondered.

Parents everywhere foster secret questions of the heart. Many struggle to understand why one or more children travel such peculiar life paths. Sometimes a child strays so far from family dreams that parents wonder if the child belongs in another galaxy, or whether a switch took place in the delivery room. Wide variances in personality occur frequently in families. These differences defy the "All Alike" myth. Why do such distinct variations predictably occur?

**NEW AND IMPROVED BELIEF 4
CHILDREN STRIVE
FOR UNIQUE IDENTITIES**

Each child strives to establish a place of significance in the family. Usually a child wishes to be "best" at something, whether the best is being good or being bad. Have you ever overheard a child brag, "I am the second best student in my family"? Being second best earns little notoriety. The influence of ordinal position and sibling rivalry on the creation of identity fascinated parents long before Alfred Adler and Walter Toman first investigated the sibling rivalry for uniqueness. However, Adler and Toman's work greatly influenced our understanding of family ordination. Their work contributes significantly to New and Improved Belief #4.

> **Usually a child wishes to be "best" at something, whether the best is being good or being bad.**

Personality characteristics form when children divide the family turf. Where one child succeeds, others will not follow unless both parents model specific values and traits. The children of highly competitive parents differ the most in personality, because each sibling feels the need to excel in order to be worthy of note.

At times, one child may believe that all of the positive identities belong to the other siblings. In these cases a youngster may choose to become best at being bad. Although parents may add to the discouragement of a child, they never enjoy total influence over the situation. Children, not parents, carve out their personalities as they compete for the family turf.

First and second children close in age most clearly display turf division. Their splitting of the turf leads to the major rule for the personalities of first and second children: They will be OPPOSITES. Exceptions occur only where family values exist. How first and second children divide the turf differs from family to family. But I have noticed that the following turf divisions frequently appear:

> One moves by logic; the other by the wind.
> One creates laughter; the other brings tears.
> One counts achievements; the other counts friends.
> One collects valuables; the other gives them away.
> One conforms to rules; the other to feelings.
> One enjoys neatness; the other relishes clutter.
> One works independently; the other by committee.
> One helps others; the other asks for help.
> One excels in school; the other outside of class.
> One dresses conservatively; the other forgets to dress.
> One becomes idealistic; the other worldly.
> One keeps family secrets; the other broadcasts them.
> One solves problems diplomatically; the other by tantrums.

Even when strong family values lead each child to share one area of strength, such as academic success, children will adopt different specialties. One becomes best in history, while another chooses English, and still another, mathematics. Children close to each other in age strive to create uniqueness, not similarities.

Children often follow typical patterns. One I refer to as the Scholar-Artist Split. The Maxwell family displayed this common division of turf between first and second children. The Maxwells initially entered our parent study program because of incessant fighting between their two daughters, Marcia (12) and Marie (10). As time passed the parents' concern shifted to the growing gulf between the children's personalities. For the Maxwells, Marcia's and Marie's extreme differences led to those parental questions of the heart that foster guilt and anxiety.

Mrs. Maxwell described each child: "Marcia loves school and works hard to make exceptional grades. Despite the fact that we praise Marcia for her grades, Marie shows no motivation to receive similar attention. Marcia helps around the house and rarely violates family rules. She always controls herself, except around Marie, who constantly picks on her. Marcia visits her grandparents and generally makes everyone happy.

"On the other hand Marie ignites the world. She rarely studies, and she creates anxiety and excitement all of the time. Marie's primary interests seem to be dance and music lessons. She dislikes rules and basically does what she pleases. Marie's bedroom looks like Atilla the Hun ransacked it. She rarely appears to care about the rest of the family's happiness; yet she enjoys more friends than any of us. Basically, Marie blossoms outside of our house and causes turmoil inside."

When the Scholar-Artist Split occurs, the older child assumes a more traditional, conservative identity. Then the second develops a fiery, creative temperament. But turf can be divided in many ways. The only steadfast rule remains: First and second children create opposite personalities.

The Hinsons experienced an entirely different turf

> **When the Scholar-Artist Split occurs, the older child assumes a more traditional, conservative identity. Then the second develops a fiery, creative temperament. But turf can be divided in many ways.**

division. John and Peggy Hinson entered counseling because of their eight-year-old son's academic problems. In the first session Jason slumped deeply into his chair. A serious, almost painful, expression creased his face. His speech was slow and deliberate. Across the room his six-year-old sister, Emily, danced in her seat. Eyes sparkling, she actively participated in conversation and displayed a lovely, winsome personality. When asked how she liked school, Emily replied: "Oh, I love it. It's so much fun. I have lots of friends, and I am in an advanced reading class." The parents beamed with pride. Meanwhile Jason stared at the floor, slumping further into his seat.

In the Hinson home the early turf battle ended in total victory for Emily. By becoming too powerful for Jason, Emily, with little opposition, conquered the territory she desired. Emily left Jason vanquished and disoriented. His discouragement weighed heavily on his parents, and because of the "All Alike" myth, the parents mistakenly assumed total responsibility. Although their parental training failed to equip them to handle such a one-sided turf war, the major problem occurred because of the precocious Emily's domination of positive positions. Jason proved best only in experiencing school problems.

Other ordinal positions frequently assume predictable features. Youngest children often become the Family Pride Child. Something special flows from a youngest's personality. Because they live in a world of giants, the youngest usually feels the least competent. Nevertheless, they become the most ambitious, wishing to catch up with their elders. The climb to the top of the sibling mountain appears long, strenuous and potentially perilous. To facilitate their climb, the youngest develop enchanting qualities, including humor and gamesmanship.

Both inside and outside of the home, the youngest entertain and charm others. They generally establish friendships easily and win people to their corner. In

> **Something special flows from a youngest's personality.**

addition to charm and originality, the youngest soon specialize in playing the system.

By becoming helpless when with those who love to help, the youngest always find assistance. They provide cheer for the cheerless and authority for the directionless. While on one hand learning to please authority figures, they also successfully guide the weak. The youngest tend to accept responsibility only for tasks they wish to perform. Most dislike meddling with details or uninteresting work. Their attitude may reflect an "all or nothing" stance. As a result, youngest children become either the best in certain areas and tasks, or they refuse to lift a finger. Usually, youngest children remain close to those whose interest is strong in tending to the details required for daily living.

An only child strikes others as An Already Grown Child. Living primarily with adults, the only child matures quickly. Because adult conversations appeal to the only child, he prefers the company of adults. The only child does not divide turf. He owns it.

This lack of sibling rivalry for identity allows a strong sense of security to develop. However, parents must encourage interactions with other children. Cooperation and communication skills develop with practice. Lack of involvement with other children delays a child's growth in these areas. An only child generally prospers in school and in professional life. Such children are achievers. With enriching early experiences, including opportunities to interact with peers, they also develop positive relationships.

The child who enters the family long after the births of other siblings is often a surprise addition. In my book, *Parenting Without Guilt*, I nickname this child the Whoops Child. If the parents consider this child to be a special blessing to their later years, the Whoops Child transforms into the Jehovah's Gift Child.

Raised by both parents and older siblings, the Whoops

Child's every move fascinates the family. While often a strong achiever, the Whoops Child becomes a super only-youngest combination. Because of the family's enthrallment with the unexpected child, outsiders must be careful before offering criticism. After all, a gift from Jehovah deserves no earthly appraisal. Nevertheless, a Whoops Child usually overcomes early pampering and adjusts well to life's demands.

Middle children of three develop second child characteristics, but often suffer from strong feelings that life is not fair. Most often their sentiment is founded on some basis of truth. Middle children share neither the privileges of the oldest nor the special attention of the youngest. The best situation for a middle child is to be the only boy or girl in the family. But if this is not the case, the battle for significance becomes the hardest of any ordinal position.

Middle children in families with four or more children follow trends less predictably. Some theorists believe the third child in large families possesses the most precarious position. If the third child senses that problems exist in the parents' marriage, extreme behaviors may be engaged in to reunite parents through their concern for the child. Others suggest that one sibling, often the fourth child, becomes a systems analyst. This child interprets and analyzes the symbolic meaning of each member's behavior and shares the analysis with the rest of the family.

In my work with families, I have discovered that middle children tend to divide the same territory repeatedly. Forming their own sibling cliques, large families appear to spawn several mini-constellations, each including — at the least — a first and second child. Generally, mini-constellations include children closest in age. Middle children of large families usually cooperate well and appear less demanding than the first, second and youngest children. Never accustomed to being the center of attention, middle children learn to interact and work with people of all ages.

> **Middle children of three . . . suffer from strong feelings that life is not fair. Most often their sentiment is founded on some basis of truth.**

In most cases, parental involvement has less influence on a child's choice of personality than the striving to earn a special place among brothers and sisters. Children in the same family strive to be different, not similar.

"Mrs. Jones, your children are so much alike." Only strangers and childless couples could fall for this myth. Parents who abide by the "All Alike" myth soon experience shock when their children begin to differ significantly. Should a child's striving for identity carry him outside of the boundaries of parental expectations and dreams, adults may develop self-doubts and personal feelings of failure. But in most cases, parental involvement has less influence on a child's choice of personality than the striving to earn a special place among brothers and sisters. Children in the same family strive to be different, not similar.

**NEW PITFALL 4
SECOND CHILDREN
ARE ALL ALIKE**

"A little knowledge is a dangerous thing" holds true for predicting children's unique personalities. Everything can be different, psychologists correctly suggest. Many factors alter the striving for uniqueness. For example, the death of a child complicates turf division. Even children who die at birth still live in the parents' memory, often becoming idealized. If parents openly or indirectly attribute the most positive position to the absent child, the remaining children become discouraged by an unbeatable ghost child.

A child's illness early in life often results in understandable pampering which complicates the sibling rivalry for turf. Childhood illness by necessity allows a child special attention. Other children must work harder to gain recognition. Some may grow discouraged and resent the sick child's special place.

Stepfamilies face many interesting challenges when they merge two sets of children. In these situations, a stepfamily may end up with two oldest, two middle and two youngest children. Rivalries for power and position usually follow. Sometimes these conflicts involve two teams of natural siblings. It requires time and patience for stepchildren to build a new position of significance in the family.

As in the case of the Hinsons, a perfect child (one perceived as perfect, that is) is a curse to other siblings. Any child who has many positive attributes leaves the others struggling to find positive turf. If a perfect child gains too much power, another child may be pushed out of the "litter" — unable to find a positive identity.

Age also influences the sibling rivalry for identity. Children must be close in age to be in the same constellation of influence. Any break of four years between two children creates families with mini-constellations. Another significant factor mentioned above involves the family values modeled by both parents and often shared by each child.

The search for a unique identity assures parents that children will create divergent personalities. So many variables influence the division of turf that generalizations often misfire. To pigeonhole a child by saying, for example, "He acts just like a second child" hinders a child. When parents expect specific negative behaviors of *any* child, the youngster soon conforms to the expectations. Such "self-fulfilling prophesies" endanger a child's freedom.

Yes, children in a family seek unique identities, but their selection of turf depends on a host of factors, not all of which parents control. Don't assume the burden of total responsibility for your child's characteristics, because parents provide only one among many influences in a child's personality formation.

> **Don't assume the burden of total responsibility for your child's characteristics, because parents provide only one among many influences in a child's personality formation.**

MYTH 5

ALL CHILDREN NEED IS LOVE

An old tune suggests that "you always hurt the one you love."

Good parents most often hurt their children because of their misguided attempts to motivate them. Loving parents want their children to develop all of their abilities and potential. However, love alone does not promote self-actualization. Parents choose techniques they hope will inspire growth, but often choices bring unfortunate results.

Dwelling on children's shortcomings, Destructive Motivators believe that constructive criticism inspires. The opposite is true. Criticism is the cancer of the spirit. Steady doses of negativism eat away children's enthusiasm. Soon the child becomes an empty shell, devoid of the courage needed to self-actualize. Discouraged children abandon growth for safety.

Not-Good-Enoughers and Not-Quite-Righters love children but discourage them. Not-Good-Enoughers promote an overall feeling of failure. Parts of a child's efforts seem fine, but the whole falls short. Not-Quite-Righters become parental critics who expose a child's

> Dwelling on children's shortcomings, Destructive Motivators believe that constructive criticism inspires. The opposite is true.

flaws. Implying that the whole may be adequate, they nevertheless criticize each of the parts. As a result, children lose confidence.

Glenda and Mark Bessimer were Not-Good-Enoughers. Their love for their only son Murray, age 13, was unquestionable. Nevertheless, whatever Murray accomplished was never good enough. In their first counseling session the Bessimers complained about Murray's behavior in school, his study habits, personal hygiene, tendency to lie, table manners, lack of respect for authority, and on and on.

Glenda Bessimer particularly expressed disappointment with her son. After her list of dissatisfactions drew to a close, I asked her to list two things Murray did acceptably. After thinking for a moment, she responded, "I really cannot think of any."

Amazed, I asked her to INVENT one compliment a day to share with Murray. The next week she returned to report her failure: "I couldn't think of any positive comments. I tried, but there aren't any." For Mrs. Bessimer, only perfection merited acknowledgement. Her criticisms strangled Murray's spirit. Discouraged, he stopped trying to succeed. The less he succeeded, the more critical his mother became. Alas, the discouraging circle continued.

Soon Glenda followed with a story often shared by discouraging parents: "When I was a girl, my mother never said anything positive about me. I never felt confident. Now it's hard for me to say positive things. I know I should, but I can't. I have the same problem with my friends, and on the job. I just can't be positive. And to be honest, I see little to be positive about."

Away from his parents, Murray displayed positive traits. In sessions, I complimented him, hoping that his parents might pick up on leads. But they never did. On their last visit, Mrs. Bessimer complained: "It annoys me that Murray enjoys these visits. He becomes very excited

Dad never understood: "I just don't understand Tommy's lack of interest in anything." Actually, Tommy lost interest in being pelted by "constructive criticism."

on appointment days. I fear you may mislead him into believing he's doing well. He tries to impress you. Of course, he shows his true colors outside of your office." The Bessimers never caught on. My attempts to help Murray and the Bessimer family fell short. Of course, the Bessimers would have it no other way! Not-Good-Enoughers raised by discouraging parents pass negativism to another generation. They love children, but love is not enough.

Not-Quite-Righters find fault with details, nitpicking children's courage away. Despite the circumstances, parental snipers take pot shots at every performance. Although adults camouflage their pettiness by calling it "constructive criticism," nothing constructive emerges.

For years, Tom Jackson looked forward to the day Tom, Jr., would be old enough to play sports. Finally, at age five, Tom, Jr., asked his dad for a basketball goal. Immediately the goal was built. But nothing satisfied the father: "No, you can't dribble with two hands." "Come on, Tom, you can throw it higher than *that*." "You've got to move your feet faster." More criticisms than basketballs filled the air. Soon Tom, Jr., left his basketball in the toy closet. No longer wanting to play with dad, Tom, Jr., preferred playing by himself. Dad never understood: "I just don't understand Tommy's lack of interest in anything." Actually, Tommy lost interest in being pelted by "constructive criticism."

Whether led by overambition or driven by past negative relationships, parents who motivate through criticism discourage children. Discouragement often continues throughout adulthood as individuals search for a fault-free lifestyle. For example, many perfectionists grew up in homes with critical parents. To avoid criticism, young perfectionists strive to be beyond reproach. Unfortunately, many model their parents' skill for faultfinding. Soon they too expect perfection of themselves and others.

Requiring perfectly clean homes, perfectly disciplined

children, and other impossibilities, perfectionists draw children's attention away from experimentation and expansion. To appear perfect, one narrows the world and avoids serendipity. Perfectionists create a controlled, anxious world and pass it to their children.

Self-doubters also experienced childhood relationships filled with criticism. Self-doubters hesitate in life, never confident in their judgment. They ask authority figures for continuous approval. Endorsement provides an insurance policy against criticism. Otherwise outstanding graduate students ask repeatedly: "Is this idea O.K.?" "How should I handle this situation?" "What do you think I should do in the event that . . ." Self-doubters still believe someone watches over their shoulder, waiting to catch them in an error. To avoid criticism, they require others to assume responsibility for decisions. Self-doubters fear life's unpredictability.

Self-doubt may cause a child to declare "ability bankruptcy." Alfred Adler, the founder of Individual Psychology, believed that such children assume disabilities which provide insulation from failure. By not working in school, they default, rather than lose. Their failure comes because of noncompliance, not poor work. Believing their work would fail, these children assume disabilities to avoid criticism. They turn in no assignments. Perfectionists and those with assumed, rather than real disabilities create stances that avoid criticism. Neither displays courage. Both hide from the risks of living.

Many adults assume a stance supportive of children but employ an occasional negative technique. For example, making comparisons always seem to blow up in a parent's face. Unless a child exhibits strong confidence before such comparison, discouragement increases afterwards.

Recently a mother told me in the presence of her children; "Johnny isn't as popular with the kids as his sister is. He never has been. But he's really a wonderful child,

Self-doubters still believe someone watches over their shoulder, waiting to catch them in an error.

and I think others would love him if he tried harder to know them." Johnny's mother secretly wanted to support Johnny and encourage him to try harder. But her method broadcast his weaknesses and intensified his discouragement. Comparisons between siblings in regard to grades, housework, sports ability, personality, and other areas carries destructive potential. Children know their weaknesses. Negative comparison inspires only highly motivated children, already confident in their ability to succeed.

Adults should understand the fallacy of making comparisons from their own experiences. How would a new spouse respond to this comparison? "You really don't kiss as well as my first wife. But if you applied yourself, I know you could improve." Telling a child or adult he "could do better with more effort" discourages. It suggests one can't even live up to oneself. Being compared less favorably to another destroys any remaining motivation.

Some comparisons cause children to be overshadowed by the accomplishments of a parent. During his early years, Mr. St. Lawrence won his state's amateur golf championship. Afterwards, he won many regional tournaments and placed well in several national events. As an adult, he displayed his trophies prominently throughout the house. Tales of his triumphs filled conversation hours. His son, Jerry, aspired to follow Dad's example.

Jerry won his age group's city championships and soon became highly regarded on the state level. After high school, Jerry played collegiate golf, but never reached his father's national notoriety. Golfers respected Jerry; however, Jerry never felt successful. Being raised in a shrine dedicated to his father's conquests left Jerry with a lasting impression of inadequacy. Mr. St. Lawrence's shadow loomed too large over Jerry for him to find light of his own.

Unlike comparisons, guilt trips often propel children toward their parents' goals, but usually enjoyment dimin-

How would a new spouse respond to this comparison? "You really don't kiss as well as my first wife. But if you applied yourself, I know you could improve."

ishes and resentment abounds. When children do what they "should" do, they are driven rather than self-motivated. Fritz Perls, founder of Gestalt Therapy, described such victims of guilt as people who "should all over themselves."

Moralizations flow from some parents: "You should love to visit Grandmom. After all, she's very sick and old." Or: "If you loved God enough, you would enjoy sitting through church services." Or: "You should love going to school. Most children in the world would exchange anything for your opportunities." Guilt-induced motivation may move a child toward parental goals; however, the side effects of anger, resentment and "should-ism" become heavy burdens.

"All children need is love." False. Children need the kind of motivation that encourages personal growth. Techniques that feature criticism, comparisons, and guilt chip away a child's courage. The proper motivation of children requires more than the good intentions of love.

NEW AND IMPROVED BELIEF 5
CHILDREN NEED
ENCOURAGEMENT

Encouragement energizes; criticism deadens. Children, like adults, respond enthusiastically to positive feedback. Encouragement, as the word suggests, gives courage to children. Courageous children repeatedly try to succeed without fearing failure. Yes, constructive criticism finds a place in the training of children. However, encouragement, not criticism, activates children's desire to grow.

Adults respond similarly. Imagine a young woman giving her first public presentation. She is nervous and anxious. Afterwards her husband remarks: "It was basi-

Encouragement energizes; criticism deadens.

cally good, BUT you spoke much too fast and were way too complex." Does this encourage the wife to speak again? Hardly. She probably remembers only those comments following the word BUT.

On the other hand, pretend a friend reported, "Your presentation was lively and fast-paced. I enjoyed hearing ideas I usually don't think about." Now the presenter is encouraged. She most likely will be willing to speak again and will work harder to enrich her presentations. Confident, she may ask how to improve her delivery. At that point, she benefits from advice.

But her husband may retort: "Yes, I understand, encouragement. However, I am not a Pollyanna. Besides, I am right. She went too fast and was too complex." Possibly the husband *is* right, but he must decide whether he prefers being right to motivating a loved one. Remember, a time and place for constructive criticism exist.

Most people possess limited natural encouraging skills. Like the Bessimers, adults adopt motivational tools learned from parents. A simple experiment should convince parents of the power of encouragement. Pick any person who is learning something new. Find positive comments to share about his or her attempts and refrain from criticism. For example, you might comment to a young child learning to write, "I like the way you make your L's." Or, to a young reader, "I enjoy the way you read with expression." Children respond with enthusiasm. Their efforts increase.

With practice, Not-Good-Enoughers and Not-Quite-Righters may adopt a supportive, encouraging stance. Instead of searching for evidence of failure, they can learn to seek signs of success. Effective teachers change cycles of failure in children by "catching them being good." Expecting success, highlighting the positive, and actively encouraging efforts, teachers lead discouraged children to achieve more positively. Likewise, parents build overall success by emphasizing small accomplishments: "I really like the way you helped your brother." Or: "I appreciate the way you cleared your dishes from the table." Or: "I am impressed by your concentration when you read the newspaper."

Children mix success with failure. Parental critics develop a keen eye for shortcomings. They expect failure and find it. Parents expecting success concentrate on the positive, thereby encouraging a child's self-confidence.

Mr. Stevenson used basketball to mend a broken relationship with his son. Like Mr. Jackson in a previous example, Mr. Stevenson once displayed love through fault-finding. Following a parenting class, Mr. Stevenson decided to try encouragement. After asking his son to shoot baskets with him, Mr. Stevenson carefully made only positive comments about Todd's rather limited ability. Todd responded enthusiastically.

The Stevensons played for a long time the first night. In the days following Todd greeted his dad with a smile and a basketball. After a few weeks, Mr. Stevenson took Todd to a college game. Along the way the two talked and began a special relationship. By dwelling on the positive, Mr. Stevenson transformed an antagonistic relationship built on criticism, into a supportive one built upon encouragement.

After a crisis which involves change or loss, children need loads of encouragement. For example, after a divorce children often feel discouraged. Indeed, they may blame themselves for the breakup of their parents' marriage. Not only do parents need to relieve their children of guilt and fears, but also they need to emphasize what their children do well in school and at home. Stepfamilies face similar challenges as their new families emerge. Children, as well as parents, will feel vulnerable. Nothing helps adults and children more than knowing that they're doing well and are appreciated.

Highly discouraged children, including those with assumed disabilities, require frequent success experi-

> **Parental critics develop a keen eye for shortcomings. They expect failure and find it. Parents expecting success concentrate on the positive, thereby encouraging a child's self-confidence.**

ences. Be careful with your expectations. Try not to allow a discouraged child to fail. For example, good teachers assign low-risk tasks to the deeply discouraged: "Take your book home tonight and just look through it for a few seconds." Small successes earn strong reinforcement. Parents may begin encouraging a child by asking for help in rather simple tasks: "Could you help me carry this table," or, "Would you mind helping me make up this bed?" Any effort to succeed needs swift acknowledgement. The more a child fails, the more success is needed as an antidote.

Parents need to model the "courage to be imperfect." Instead of demanding perfection from themselves, they can model facing setbacks with grace and humor. "I goofed!" become words of liberation for children. In a graduate class demonstration, the children appeared unusually aware of the audience. Their replies displayed an unhelpful tenseness. By accident, I spilled a little of the soft drink used in an experiment. I laughed and said, "Whoops, I goofed." The children laughed and gleefully turned to the audience to announce, "Dr. West goofed." Everyone enjoyed the error; the children relaxed, and their performances improved. Everyone makes mistakes. Children need to know it's no "big deal."

With practice, adults succeed in actively avoiding the use of comparisons. Soon parents also minimize the effect of unsolicited comparisons. Notice the faces of children when someone compliments one child and not the others. Countenances fall. "Mrs. Burch, your daughter is such a good athlete. You must be tremendously proud of her." Soon parents respond, "Yes, all of my children enjoy athletics." Smiles appear. Everyone feels encouraged. Children know that differences exist among them, but comparisons create rifts.

Mutual respect eliminates guilt trips. By accepting your children's feelings, you display your respect for emotions that differ from yours. Model your beliefs and

Parents need to model the "courage to be imperfect."

trust your modeling's power to influence your children's major values. True, children must do things they would prefer not to do, but parents need not bully them into professing enjoyment. Being critical of children's emotions leads them to hide their feelings or resist cooperation. If overpowered by the temptation to say something, compliment a child's friend who participates in the activity in question, "I love the way Graham enjoys helping his mother cook." Make the comment admiringly, not comparatively. Sometimes children respond to encouragement, even directed to peers.

Love is not enough. Misguided love snuffs the spirit of a child and discourages. Instead, nourish the spirit by helping children feel that they can succeed at anything. Use the miracle technique: encouragement.

NEW PITFALL 5
NEVER CRITICIZE A CHILD

There exists a proper time, place and method to share constructive criticism. Remember that children experience feelings similar to those of adults. When do adults accept criticism best? Most would respond, "Never." Among the most inappropriate occasions are crises, periods of personal discouragement, or in the presence of others. Whenever a child performs tasks which require risk, a crisis exists. Children wonder: Will anyone like my work? Will I be successful? A parent's most important task is to support the child's interest. Later, adults can create opportunities for sharing constructive criticism.

Mr. Webb looked at his son Larry's shop project. Larry's face beamed with pride. Obvious defects appeared and Mr. Webb was tempted to point them out. Instead, he encouraged: "I am so pleased you enjoy

Constructive criticism plays a role in helping children gain competency. But like a lethal drug, in large quantities and at the wrong time, it is a killer.

working with tools. I love seeing your results." Later in the week Mr. Webb asked Larry to help construct a small project. As they worked, Mr. Webb mixed compliments with occasional advice on how to ADD to Larry's skill. Larry was thrilled. Each attempt at something new brought encouragement from the father.

Never teach during a crisis. Wait until a special time when a child can try your suggestions and receive your support. Whenever you observe the slightest progress, acknowledge it. Nothing builds enthusiasm and confidence like encouragement. Constructive criticism plays a role in helping children gain competency. But like a lethal drug, in large quantities and at the wrong time, it is a killer.

MYTH 6

PARENTS CAN NEVER DO TOO MUCH FOR THEIR CHILDREN Few parents fall hook, line and sinker for this myth. But when they do, all of society suffers the consequences. If you teach in public schools, you encounter childhood victims of this myth daily. The rest of us know them well but often avoid them. Nevertheless, we all learn something from parents who wander to extremes in raising children.

At first it may seem strange to consider that pampered and neglected children's parents fall prey to the same myth. But in both cases parents believe or act as if they cannot give too much to their children. Indulgent adults contribute *too much of everything.* Neglectful parents allow *too much freedom.*

Monsters of the Classroom — Given Too Much of Everything

Treated like royalty early in life, Monsters of the Classroom expect to get what they want when they want it. Every toy your own child saves for, these pampered princes carelessly leave littered across their homes and yards. Living atop a geyser of perpetual toys and special privileges, these super-getters develop an insatiable appetite for possessions and advantage.

What earned these children their regal rights? No one knows for sure. But at some point, one parent or both launched the Prince and Princess Syndrome by becoming overinvolved with a child. Based on the sinister myth that "parents can never do too much for their children," these parents created monsters by overgiving and overdoing for their children. In the process, these parents robbed their children of the opportunity to develop independence, self-confidence and cooperation. In exchange for pampering, princely children treat parental benefactors with disrespect and contempt. When special privileges are given too frequently, the child's heart shrinks and all gratitude seems squeezed out. The Royal Children become Super Babies who fail to grow in the specific areas of their parents' excessive pampering.

Super Babies slide through the years continuing to display the areas abused by overindulgence. For example, as adults some Perpetual Babies display the Reverse Midas Touch—everything touched turns to trash. Within ten minutes after contact, rooms the Perpetual Babies entered become hazardous waste sites, cars turn into four-wheeled Dempsey Dumpsters, and offices arouse laughter from the sternest OSHA agents.

Parental maids created these garbage-laden humans by demanding little of them. Whenever the Super Baby created a mess, someone followed with a broom. Parents accepted and robbed the child of responsibility for caring for bedrooms, possessions and other property. As an adult, the now Helpless Giant must discover a spouse willing to continue domestic servitude.

Parental disregard for building a child's responsibility varies. By intervening in fights, parents rob a child of the

> **In exchange for pampering, princely children treat parental benefactors with disrespect and contempt.**

ability to solve controversy. Entering conflicts between a child and other adults — such as teachers, neighbors, or administrators — prevents the young from learning to handle authority. Instead, children depend on others during times of crisis even when they become adults. An example appears in Yo-Yo Marriages where a child-adult summons parents to mediate in marital squabbles. Why can't the young adults solve their own problems? Because their parents always settled conflicts for them.

Smaller areas of dependency develop because of lack of exposure. Some fail to learn to choose and buy clothing. Others develop tool-helplessness and can fix nothing around the house. Financial disabilities grow in children who have never been expected to save or manage personal money. Most people experience weaknesses in some areas of living. Super Babies become dependent in too many areas to achieve autonomy and self-confidence

Interestingly, after receiving the objects of their demands for so many years, Super Babies believe that privileges have become rights. They want what they want when they want it, and they feel mistreated if they do not receive it. If denied, Super Babies throw temper tantrums and/or depressions at the villains who mistreated them. Historically, emotional blackmail paid off because parents of princely children often submitted to intimidation.

For example, on how many occasions have you watched a child in a department store wailing over a denied candy bar? At first the parent stands firm, "No!" Tantrums follow from the pampered child. The next time the child appears, his face is stuffed with chocolate, and a finger points to the next object of his insatiable desires.

Many situations make adults particularly vulnerable to overdoing for a child. Single parents may "feel sorry" for the child. A few stepparents attempt to win the love of their stepchildren by giving in to their every wish. Children who endure long bouts with illness or have mental or physical handicaps may be pampered excessively. Although all of these parental reactions are understandable, overindulgence never helps a child.

Tyrants of the stores become Monsters of the Classrooms. For most children of princely background, teachers become the first authority figures outside of the kingdom. Monsters of the Classroom demand a disproportionate amount of a teacher's energy. Never satisfied to be one of 25 students, they require undue amounts of attention, time and praise. Often teachers are the first to say no to the child with uncompromising conviction. How unfair this denial seems to a Super Baby. Rage follows.

If teachers complain, parents respond: "I can't believe my child would do that. His behavior at home is perfect!" And, of course, it probably is. As long as a cook, chauffeur, body guard and maid service are there for him, there is little reason to complain. As Super Babies grow older, they find few opportunities to rebel. In firm possession of Dad's (or their own) car, gas money, a generous allowance and promises to pay future college bills, adolescents encounter little opposition. Problems occur only when an authority opposes their will, or failures in life begin to take place.

For example, motivational difficulties may appear in school subjects where little interest or success occurs. Years on Easy Street failed to prepare many adolescents to overcome distasteful challenges. Parents respond to their beloved's school problems with uncertainty; they alternate between handling the problem with bribery or creating strong restrictions. Neither works. Super Babies generally own everything they want: therefore studying for dollars is unappealing. Also parents' lack of familiarity with setting limits leads to failure in restricting the child.

Parents bring pampered kids to counseling after bribes and restrictions fail to increase motivation. The Jacksons brought Tina, their youngest child by 12 years, to counseling because of academic failings. At age 12, Tina received a swimming pool for her birthday. In her

---

Often teachers are the first to say no to the child . . . How unfair this denial seems to a Super Baby. Rage follows.

opinion, not another decent gift appeared until her sixteenth birthday, at which time her parents finally presented her with a car. During her junior year of high school, Tina experienced her first academic difficulty. The Jacksons responded by booking a summer tour to Europe for her as an incentive to improve.

Tina studied less, however, and her parents pressured her more. But studying was unpleasant, and it was "not where I'm at," said Tina. Where she was "at" was out late at night with other Super Babies — cruising out of control.

Desperate, her parents grounded her. Not being skilled in the art of discipline, they failed to make their decision stick. Tina routinely left home in violation of agreements. Hurt, the parents felt unappreciated and unloved. Predictably, Tina shared these same feelings toward them. To Tina, her parents' restrictions seemed harsh and heartless. Because she believed the rules to be unreasonable, Tina simply refused to obey them.

When the Jacksons escorted Tina to their first counseling session, the parents' first queries were, "What's wrong with Tina? She was perfect until she turned 16," and, "Can you get her grades up for her?" No quick magic cures a lifetime of pampering.

During adolescence Super Babies rarely grow unless life delivers an unexpected conflict. By their 30s they become Super Brats. From a nonroyal vantage point it appears Super Brats enjoy every advantage in life. But the chorus from the pampered monsters resounds: "We are bored. There must be more to life."

Why are they bored? Because they are getters who no longer "get" increasingly exciting rewards. Several famous athletes of our day display this super bratdom. Their well known attempts to solve boredom include bouts with drugs, crime, sexual exploitation and more.

Getters rarely discover giving. Traditionally adults achieve meaning through focusing on contributing to a

> **During adolescence Super Babies rarely grow unless life delivers an unexpected conflict. By their 30s they become Super Brats.**

new generation. But for Championship Getters, giving to others remains an undeveloped art.

The final irony for the pampered child comes with the realization of death's inevitability. To them, death appears to be the most obvious imperfection in God's flawed creation. Because death knows no exceptions, it cannot be escaped by the use of tantrums, depression, or bribes. Super Brats run swiftly from death, but escape becomes one gift they cannot "get."

Street Corner Terrorists Given Too Much Freedom

Another set of those who want everything NOW come from different origins. Unlike pampered princes, these children experience little parental involvement. To avoid the inconvenience of raising children, a few parents create young Street Corner Terrorists by allowing them total freedom with no life structure.

The opposite of Super Babies, these childhood survivors learn self-responsibility early. Many awaken themselves, fix breakfast or eat nothing, then journey to school, if they wish. At night they wander the streets without restriction.

These graduates of the streets create their own guidelines, values and goals. Their usual goals are focused on obtaining daily happiness. Future plans remain tentative or unrealistic, but confidence exists that future challenges will be handled with finesse.

Adults living in children's bodies are victims of neglect who present an unfair challenge for schools. Seldom are teachers equipped to handle the powerful emotions of these adult children who are accustomed to following their own rules. Because the curriculum is irrelevant to their immediate desires, these children become uninterested in the gifts of education.

Street-wise children soon fail in the classroom. As

To avoid the inconvenience of raising children, a few parents create young Street Corner Terrorists by allowing them total freedom with no life structure.

failures, these outcasts feel like prisoners in an institution that celebrates academic success. Soon child terrorists pit their street skills against the school's authority to imprison them. The young terrorists of the street corners may even become tyrants of the bathroom. In one local school, a second-grade terrorist charged other children 25 cents to leave the bathroom. But as he quipped, "At least I didn't charge kids to enter."

Misbehavior grows common: smoking in the bathrooms, cherry bombs flushed down toilets, smashed-in lockers. Schools become a battleground. The school defenses seem unfit for response. Traditional discipline techniques prove useless. Schools threaten to fail students who are already failing. By suspending students who prefer the streets, authorities bring to mind Brer Rabbit's being thrown into the briar patch. Finally, principals complain to disinterested parents who have relinquished all control long ago.

Occasionally, schools gather the worst of the street children in classes for the "emotionally disturbed." A few truly disturbed children accompany the street kids to justify the classification. But even elementary school kids know that these children are not emotionally disturbed but are emotionally disturbing to teachers unaccustomed to "unmotivated students."

Unmotivated, however, is educational jargon meaning, "they won't do what we want them to do." Street children exhibit a high motivation to do what they want to do when they want to do it. Although occasionally a gifted principal or teacher versed in encouragement converts a child, most eventually flush out of the system as time passes.

Studies show that when school days end the self-concepts of many Street Corner Terrorists improve. Away from failure and threats, some youth find contributing places in society. But a few continue or even escalate attacks against others and, often, against their own bodies.

> **Unmotivated, however, is educational jargon meaning, "they won't do what we want them to do."**

Street Corner Terrorists now push until something stops them. For drugs and alcohol, the body becomes the ultimate enforcer of limitations. For those perpetuating crimes against others, the police may inflict limitations if other Street Corner Terrorists don't. Usually these culprits establish a long record of court appearances. All children find limitations, but for some the outer boundaries are too severe.

"Parents can never do too much for their children." Whether by parental design or default, this myth becomes disastrous not only to these children but to all parts of society that they touch.

NEW AND IMPROVED BELIEF 6
NEVER DO FOR A CHILD
WHAT HE CAN DO FOR HIMSELF

This improved belief suggests that parents insure that children become competent and self-confident.

Like many new, improved beliefs this one originated centuries ago and was formalized by Rudolph Dreikurs, a founder of parent education, in the 1930s. This improved belief suggests that parents insure that children become competent and self-confident. Independence-training begins early as children are expected to perform age-appropriate tasks and meet all reasonable life challenges. Children clean up their own messes, tie their own shoes, and settle their own fights. Young children often attempt skills such as pouring milk, and fail. That's O.K. They learn through setbacks to rise above frustration in life. Through encouragement they try again.

Many psychologists assert that conflict leads to growth. If children aren't given the answers to all of their questions, they discover their own answers. By being given allowances that are reasonable, children are encouraged to save for desirable toys. By completing chores in the home, young people develop household competency. By solving conflicts with siblings and friends, children become skilled in handling conflict. By meeting their school challenges independently, students become ready to succeed in later jobs. Children become SELF-controlled and SELF- motivated.

Such training requires sacrifices. Many parents retort, "It's much easier and faster if I do all of these things myself." But what saves a parent time robs a child of competency. As Dreikurs suggested, "Take time for training." Competency requires practice and success. Training by parents contributes to a child's ability. Success adds to confidence in one's competency.

What kind of children arise from the improved belief? In comparison with Super Brats, self-motivated children may appear rather docile in the classrooms. By not demanding undue attention from the teacher, self-contained children fade into the sea of cooperative faces. Self-confident children work toward realistic goals and overcome personal setbacks. Self-controlled children require little discipline and benefit from the offerings of education.

As adults, responsible children become parents easily annoyed by children at the movies who whine and cry for more candy or run unsupervised through the aisles. Adults with social interest contribute to others in a quiet, unobtrusive manner. Occasionally, superstars arise in the process. But, in a sense, any confident child or adult who does for himself is a superstar.

On the other hand, parents must do for a child what he cannot do for himself. Children cannot handle too much freedom. They require structure through reasonable limitations, supervision and assistance. Too much freedom becomes abusive to both the child and society.

Young terrorists often fall victim not only to parental neglect, but also to a society unable to meet the needs of the poor and undereducated. Street Corner Terrorists fall

> **Many parents retort, "It's much easier and faster if I do all of these things myself."**

victim to the society they later victimize. Too much of anything is seldom good. Too much freedom leads to undisciplined self-centeredness. Children struggle to survive, but in the struggle, loyalty and social consciousness too often are lost.

Unfortunately, neglectful parents may not read this book or take parenting courses. Instead, they endure in a society which makes success for them improbable and often impossible. But despite the reasons for neglect, young Street Corner Terrorists deeply need the structure and support of parents. Instead they receive too much freedom for anyone's good.

NEW PITFALL 6
OVEREXPECTATIONS AND HOME IMPRISONMENT TAKE THE JOY FROM CHILDHOOD

Overexpectations made on children's thinking and behavior rob children of joy. Overly demanding parents expect adult behavior and a competence unnatural for young children. True, they avoid pampering children, but sacrificing a childhood zest for living is the cost.

Mistakes in protocol and chores bring immediate criticism and often punishment. Questions from children find doctrinaire answers which limit creativity. Little mutuality exists in a home where parents dominate discussions and decision-making. Children are expected to be miniature adults at all times. Such homes run smoothly as long as children submit to the demands of authority. Because the atmosphere and rules of the home are made to benefit parents, at best children benefit secondarily. By trying to avoid spoiling and pampering children through demanding age-inappropriate responses to life, a few parents may tumble into New Pitfall #6.

To avoid giving too much freedom to roam, many parents give none. Protective families create thick boundaries around the home, from which no child escapes. For some children sports participation, school clubs, scouts or other extracurricular activities meet prohibition. Parents never allow children to stray from family control. Far from terrorists of the street corner, these children become smothered in the stale atmosphere of their own homes. Confined to their narrow environments, Captive Children rarely encounter the wonders in the world around them.

As a rule, extremes cause problems for children. Giving children too much creates Monsters of the Classroom and Street Corner Terrorists. Giving children too little creates Smothered Kids who must violently rebel or forever surrender the possibility of free thought and enriched experiences.

These children become smothered in the stale atmosphere of their own homes.

MYTH 7

**SPARE THE ROD
AND SPOIL THE CHILD**

"We don't hit others!" yells the mother, as her hand lands firmly on Mary's bottom. "Now remember this spanking the next time you think it's O.K. to hit your little sister." Mary cries, angry at both her mother and sister. Violent plots begin to hatch as Mary dreams of revenge.

The Slow Passage of a Myth

Our society supports two different discipline beliefs. One suggests that parents must spank children, and the other demands that parents use alternatives. The old corporal punishment myth lingers through time, a vestige of simpler days. Then, parents ruled their homesteads like Marshall Dillon ran Dodge City. Parental constables strapped on their six-guns and demanded that all problems leave town by sunset. Children retreated to the background, honoring the myth that "children should be seen and not heard."

Historically, in less complex societies, spanking forced

obedience to authority figures and conformity to parental expectations. Parents needed their children to work on family farms and businesses that would eventually be passed on to them. Free expression and imagination proved counterproductive. Crops required immediate attention, and stores prospered under close supervision. Parents passed along to their children intact beliefs about religion, politics and life — discouraging experiences which might create alternatives. Spanking kept the family system closed, which allowed families to prosper as a social and economic entity. "Spare the rod and spoil the child" remains a viable myth for families living outside of mainstream America.

Most of society left Tombstone long ago. Society changed, and new myths supported these changes. Men exchanged their six-shooters for briefcases. Women earned equality in their pursuit of educational opportunities and careers. Slaves became freedmen. Children's rights brought young people out of the mines and child labor camps. Yet, myths remain which support the old order, despite the fact that new myths and methods support society's new order.

Progress requires family change. A more complex, open society demands that children develop autonomy, initiative, and academic potential. Mutual respect and cooperation replace obedience and conformity as goals of family interaction. As a leading democracy in the world, our society emphasizes flexibility, negotiation, fairness, and logic, rather than fear and power. To meet society's demands, parents need new beliefs which emphasize clear communications and the use of educational techniques for discipline.

Old myths create havoc in special family situations. For example, stepparents who use physical punishment may face bitter resistance from their stepchildren. For stepparents to discipline children in the early years of a

> "Spare the rod and spoil the child" remains a viable myth for families living outside of mainstream America.

stepfamily's life proves to be complicated enough. But to throw gas on the fire brings explosive results.

Old myths die slowly. Like lingering prejudicial ideas about racial minorities, women and children, belief in Spanking Power still finds a comfortable home in some families. As long as families need these myths, they will survive.

Those Who Use the Rod

Many groups in our society cling to the old spanking myth. Although discipline includes many other techniques, some parents believe discipline and spanking are synonymous. No matter how effective alternatives to corporal punishment are, Disciples of the Rod maintain that "every child needs a spanking." Dedicated spankers resuscitate the myth: "Spare the rod; spoil the child." Disciples of the Rod seek no additions to their discipline weapons; therefore, they do not grow.

Many Disciples of the Rod become agnostics. Hearing about the limitations and side effects of corporal punishment, they believe better alternatives may exist; but they are trapped by their experiences. All they know is spanking. Their grandparents spanked; their parents spanked; and they follow suit. Family traditions die slowly.

For a cross-generational spanker to change discipline techniques requires initiative, courage, and education. The challenge equals that of a concert musician who wishes to play a different instrument after decades of playing only the violin. Change requires learning. Even those motivated to alter their techniques find educational opportunities sparse in the United States.

Several religious groups encourage the use of spanking. However, religious teachings mature as generations pass. For example, in recent centuries many Christians supported an Old Testament theology that directed that

All they know is spanking. Their grandparents spanked; their parents spanked; and they follow suit. Family traditions die slowly.

the hands causing sin must be cut off, or the eyes leading to immorality must be plucked out. Religious thought progressed, however, and these barbaric policies find little support in today's society.

As Christian thinking, for example, evolves, the Old Testament directive to "spare the rod and spoil the child" will be replaced by more loving New Testament notions which accent the innocence of children and the duty of the adult not to obstruct a child's growth. Eventually, Disciples of the Rod will model their parent-child relationships on the love of Jesus for mankind. Until then, a few religious groups will stagnate amidst outdated notions of discipline based on retribution and punishment.

Pragmatic Reasons to Abandon the Rod

Spanking rarely succeeds with defiant children. Tommy Jones misbehaved repeatedly during a family reunion. After ignoring many warnings, Tommy knocked down his younger cousin. Mrs. Jones grabbed Tommy's arm and issued three hard whacks across his backside. Mutinous, Tommy displayed no emotion as the spanking took place. When completed, Tommy looked toward his playmates and smiled. Off he ran to resume play with no apparent change in attitude.

Defiant children expect spankings. Knowing their parents possess no stronger medicine, obstinate children exasperate adults by accepting spankings without reaction. What can Disciples of the Rod do then? Spank harder or longer? Ironically, spanking works as a deterrent only for conforming children who fear the rod. Their compliance to rules arises, however, from fear rather than responsibility and cooperation.

Child development texts cite research suggesting that children who receive regular doses of physical punishment become sneaky. Learning outside-in morality, their attention focuses on the power of outside authority figures, rather than the development of internal moral principles. Therefore, they experience no guilt for undetected misbehaviors. Other problems occur.

George and Melba Cockran escorted their son Anthony, aged eight, to counseling. His lying exasperated them. Soon it became apparent that the Cockrans' discipline strategies relied heavily on corporal punishment. At one point Mr. Cockran shared: "When I really need to teach a lesson I use my belt. Not often, mind you. But when Anthony really needs it." I asked, "How can Anthony predict when his behavior may require a belt?" Mr. Cockran replied: "Well, he can't exactly. Of course, that keeps him on his toes. But I only use the belt when he really deserves it." After relating more stories about their frustration with Anthony's deceptions, Mrs. Cockran asked the pivotal question, "Why do you think Anthony lies?" My response appeared to hit home: "Because he is smart."

Anthony feared telling the truth. At age eight, he felt unfairly humiliated by spankings. In Anthony's view, to avoid physical punishment by any method seemed just. Lying worked well. Although the Cockrans feared that lying resulted from evil desires, in reality Anthony simply beat the spanking system.

Home atmospheres suffer when corporal punishment is relied on. Supper times provide an example. Disciples of the Rod respond to a child's eating difficulties with force: "Eat everything on your plate or else!" Children refusing to comply transform parents into "eater-beaters." After receiving a few frustrated smacks, the child sits sulking and angry. A power struggle ensues between the child's will to defy and the will of the "eater-beater" to force compliance. Tension reigns as meal times become ordeals. Alternative techniques, as we shall see, avoid

Adults who spank send a clear message: "Hitting others is acceptable under certain conditions."

these common power struggles and bring peace to the home front.

Children model behaviors of their parents. They copy their dress and mannerisms. And children imitate a parent's use of authority. Adults who spank send a clear message: "Hitting others is acceptable under certain conditions." It seems obvious to these children that a larger person in control has the right to hit others. Research in child development concludes that children who are physically punished frequently hit smaller children under their control. Children reproduce childhood experiences.

The limitations of corporal punishment arise in the common apology, "This will hurt me more than it hurts you." Discipline should hurt no one. Instead, discipline provides an opportunity for the child to learn from mistakes. Physical punishment fails to educate. Instead, it intimidates a child to conform.

Spanking opens the floodgates to potential abuse. At worst, physical punishment injures children and breaks the law. Frustration and anger generate too much momentum for some spankers. Hitting hard injures physically and often psychologically. Errors in the application of corporal punishment produce results that regret and sorrow fail to remove. No examples need be cited here. Consult your local newspaper.

Educationally, physical punishment is permissive. Children escape without taking responsibility for poor choices. Johnny Childress broke a neighbor's window. The next morning, Mrs. Childress reported to the neighbor: "I am sorry about your window. Believe me, Johnny received the whipping of his life. My husband and I will pay for your window. I don't think Johnny will ever break anything again." TOO EASY. Johnny endured a quick spanking, then accepted no further responsibility. The owner of the violated property received no apology from him. Johnny paid nothing from his allowance or

Educationally, physical punishment is permissive. Children escape without taking responsibility for poor choices.

personal savings. Spanking brought Johnny a cheap grace, unrepresentative of the demands of the "real world." As an adult, responsible reactions, not spankings, will be required from Johnny. The educational permissiveness of spanking prepares children poorly for modern adulthood.

Two myths live. Disciples of the Rod strap on six-guns, and use physical punishment to rule their territory. But a new, complex world makes tin badges and sidearms obsolete. "It hurts me more than it hurts you." What kind of discipline is that for our world? Modern parents require a new, improved belief to prepare children for responsibility.

NEW AND IMPROVED BELIEF 7
THE BEST DISCIPLINE ALLOWS CHILDREN TO EXPERIENCE THE CONSEQUENCES OF MISBEHAVIOR

"Please go to your room. Come out when you can control yourself. We do not hit others." Mary sulks off to her room, sorry — for the moment — that she helped create this rule. After several minutes Mary returns, knowing a second offense earns 15 minutes in her room, according to previous agreements.

Because children participate in establishing consequences, they accept the agreements more readily.

Children NEED discipline. The best discipline techniques prepare them for adult responsibility. Spanking offers one medicine for a variety of ailments, often producing unpleasant side-effects. By using logical and natural consequences, parents enjoy a flexible range of responses to misbehaviors. Because children participate in establishing many consequences, they accept the agreements more readily. Consequences are logical and fair; therefore, children do not fear parental authority. Creating consequences allows a family to develop an atmosphere of cooperation and mutual respect. Ironically,

Disciples of the Rod add consequences to their techniques easily. Already displaying the courage to say no, they enact consequences without hesitation.

Natural consequences allow children to learn from the results of their behaviors. Parents do not intervene. Mark zigzagged his bicycle between cars in the church's gravel parking lot. Despite a warning from mother, Mark continued. Before Mark's mother could intervene, his bicycle skidded on the loose rocks. Sliding across the gravel, Mark scraped his right knee badly. The natural consequences for Mark's stubborn behavior included a skinned knee and injured pride. Wisely, his mother said NOTHING, although she had to fight the temptation to enjoy an "I told you so." Mark's fall taught him everything he needed to know. Because Mom stayed out of the experience, Mark blamed himself. Never looking up, he mounted his bicycle and rode toward the sidewalk.

Whenever possible, allow life to teach children. In many instances, children's decisions create natural consequences that are perfect for learning. For example, in the earlier case of supper-time blues, an "eater-beater" created anxiety and tension by using physical punishment to force a child to eat. Natural consequences allow parents to influence children without direct intervention. When a child chooses not to eat, the natural consequence of this choice results in hunger. Parents need only to arrange for snacks to be unavailable during the training period.

To eat or not to eat supper becomes the child's choice. After the meal concludes, food is not available until the next morning. As the child's hunger mounts, he may demand food. Parents say only, "Breakfast is in the morning." Hungry children eat a big breakfast. Then at supper the child confronts the decision: Should I eat or not? Remembering the previous night's hunger, most children decide to eat. Parents must remain quiet during the course of training. Refrain from taunting! Allow

> **Whenever possible, allow life to teach children. In many instances, children's decisions create natural consequences that are perfect for learning.**

natural consequences to teach your child, and enjoy your supper.

Natural consequences provide discipline for a variety of situations. For example, when a child leaves without a coat, discomfort will teach future responsibility better than parental speeches will. Children who fail to care for toys either lose or break them. By not replacing broken toys, parents allow children to learn from the consequences of slovenliness. Sleeping habits also respond to natural consequences. Sleep is self-rewarding. Children who are expected to arise on time, learn to go to sleep at reasonable times. Families need to mutually establish bedtimes. At the agreed-upon time, children retire to their rooms. Parents say their "goodnights" and children put themselves to bed. At first, children experiment and stay up late; then they learn that sleep deprivation hurts. The key is to insist that children get out of bed when the alarm sounds. If parents refrain from power struggles and the temptation to say "I told you so," children naturally adjust to healthy sleep schedules.

At times, natural consequences become too severe or provide no *immediate* consequences. In these cases parents arrange logical consequences. A logical consequence requires discipline that is linked to the particular offense. Logical consequences work best when agreed upon in advance.

Parents with preteens use the "time-out" plan frequently. Children acting inappropriately go to designated areas to regain self-control. Inside the home, bedrooms may be used while, outside, steps or porches prove satisfactory. Talking to children in advance about offenses that require time-out increases cooperation. Allow children to influence decisions on time and locations.

On first offenses, families often agree to allow offenders to return of their own volition. If gaining control requires only seconds, fine. On a second offense, members return after an agreed-upon time. If a disturbance

Time-out is not punishment. It's simply what the term suggests — time out needed to gain self control.

erupts during time out, the clock is reset. Time-out is not punishment. It's simply what the term _ggests — time out needed to gain self control. Time-out works well for biting, kicking, switching televisions on and off, yelling, whining, and other socially unacceptable behaviors. Although time-out works well, parents can use a variety of consequences for the same misbehaviors.

When children misuse crayons, pens, scissors, knives or other potentially destructive objects, the tools in question should be taken from them. Messes need to be cleaned up by the child. If a child damages objects that belong to others, allowances can be tapped to pay for replacements. Children's failure to do chores may require parents to complete those jobs instead of using that time to take children to practices or other enjoyable engagements.

Logical consequences made with the help of children particularly facilitate working with teens. For example, families may set curfews by dickering back and forth until a compromise is reached. After explaining why missed curfews upset them, parents may ask, "What do you think should happen if you are late?" Teens usually create reasonable consequences, although negotiation may be required. All children accept consequences better, if they have a voice in creating them.

Consequences in regard to finances prepare teens for independence. Reasonable allowances and jobs help teens pay for their own gasoline bills, buy extra food, purchase clothes, and help toward entertainment expenses. Financial decisions soon become challenging. For example sometimes name-brand shoes must be sacrificed if money is needed for concert tickets. Any problems that arise can be discussed in family meetings, as we shall see later.

Raising children in a complex world requires new and improved beliefs and practices. Logical and natural consequences have existed for decades. Our culture finally caught up with the idea. Families who employ logical and natural consequences, build mutual respect, cooperation and responsibility. Children raised with the use of mutually made consequences view their parents as fair, while parents find children to be assertive and responsible. When parents make mistakes in utilizing consequences, results rarely harm the child. The use of natural and logical consequences create few, if any, negative side-effects.

"Spare the rod and spoil the child." Nonsense. Discipline children to live in today's world.

NEW PITFALL 7A THERE IS NOTHING WORSE THAN SPANKING Many parents suffer Discipline Disabilities. For these parents, spanking remains the single technique they understand and feel comfortable using. To abandon spanking would leave many without any response to their child's misbehavior. On the whole, permissiveness and neglect create more difficulties than an OCCASIONAL spanking. New beliefs and techniques suggest that children fare BEST with the use of good communications and logical consequences. Many children raised by the spanking myth live contributive and meaningful lives. Their success occurs, in part, because of their parents' love, encouragement, and limit-setting, *not because of spanking*. Until new ideas reign in our culture, some families will suffer the limitations of living by an antiquated myth. Nevertheless, old myths rarely survive without some need.

NEW PITFALL 7B NATURAL AND LOGICAL CONSEQUENCES REMOVE ALL MISBEHAVIOR No discipline technique removes misbehavior. But new techniques that respond to misbehavior can be used to *reduce* occurrences.

MYTH 8

"I MUST MAKE MY CHILD SUCCEED IN SCHOOL" Children's school problems challenge the most positive home atmospheres. How innocent the myth sounds: "I must make my child succeed in school," but how destructive overinvolvement becomes.

For each parent a fine line exists that separates needed parental interest and influence from parental over-involvement and force. When parents cross over this line they enter the Twilight Zone of Negative Returns, where good intentions create negative results. The more parents try to control their child, the less control they have. Everything backfires. When in the Twilight Zone, parents entangle themselves in a child's school challenges, be-coming hopelessly overinvolved. Power struggles follow. The family atmosphere sours, and performance in school usually deteriorates.

Some parents choose to shadow their child through the school years. Others are lured into overinvolvement by weak teachers, but in either case parents believe they must MAKE their child succeed.

Particularly devastating to family life are teachers who

> **The more parents try to control their child, the less control they have. Everything backfires.**

are unable to handle a child's problems independently and within the classroom. Although most teachers, despite bad press, perform their jobs beautifully, a few rotten apples drift to the bottom of the teaching barrel. Personnel problems within schools escalate parental overinvolvement.

Those who teach poorly lack at least two major skills. They fail to excite and motivate students, and they cannot provide discipline without help from others. Not able to succeed independently, these bottom-of-the-barrel professionals eventually demand that parents intervene. Parents who accept the challenge may set themselves up for failure.

Adults tolerate in teachers professional weaknesses that they would not accept from business employees. No adult would tolerate a broker's report such as this: "I know you entrusted your money to me to invest, but my investment schemes aren't working. It's your money. Tell me what you expect me to do with it to make a profit."

Without myths that create anxiety and guilt, parents would respond with anger to this kind of confession of incompetence; but when an unskilled teacher reports an inability to motivate or discipline a child, parents feel responsible and assume that they should intervene. In doing so, many spend years wandering through the Twilight Zone of Negative Returns.

Adults tolerate in teachers professional weaknesses they would not accept from business employees.

Parental Homework Custodians

Homework can spoil the atmosphere of the best of homes. Parents can provide the rules and environment which encourage a child to complete homework, but they usually fail when MAKING a child complete homework. Homework should challenge and excite the child, and often teachers fail in making assignments do this. Too many dish out homework that becomes repetitious and boring. After working a long day in school, children never wish to come home to "more of the same." Completing unchallenging homework is like doing the dishes, only to find another stack of dirty utensils still to be done. Little enthusiasm emerges for doing more of the same un-challenging work. As some doctors point out, the brain is an organ that tires, not a muscle that grows stronger with repeated repetitions.

Children rightfully resent placing their minds through useless gymnastics. Teachers unable to create interesting homework often imply that parents should FORCE children to complete mindless assignments. If parents accept this challenge, the School Disaster Syndrome begins. Homework often becomes the first domino to fall, as the following story demonstrates.

Johnny returns from school with 15 math problems similar to the 30 completed earlier in the day. Johnny's parents begin their interrogation: "Do you have any homework?" Wanting some time to play, Johnny replies, "Not much." Dissatisfied with his response, Johnny's well-meaning parents attempt to force immediate com-pliance, "Well, you MUST finish your homework before you go outside."

Having no motivation to do "more of the same," Johnny wastes time in his room feeling imprisoned by his work. Anger grows toward his homework custodians and Johnny thinks: I hate school. They can't make me do this homework. The first domino falls.

A power struggle ensues. Then, parents grow more insistent: "We planned to go out for ice cream tonight, but we won't go until Johnny finishes his homework." Everyone in the family is now under Johnny's control. Like Uncle Remus' Tar Baby, Johnny sits obstinately in his room. The struggle continues until Johnny's parents have all four feet firmly stuck.

Determined not to give in, Johnny doesn't do his work, and the family stays home. Angry parents send

Johnny to his room with orders not to exit until he completes the chore. After five minutes Johnny reports, "I am through." Suspicious parents demand an inspection, and catch Johnny in his lie. Another domino falls, and the trip into the Twilight Zone is well underway.

Never destroy a positive atmosphere at home because of assigned homework. Keep the importance of homework in perspective. Quality teachers create interesting homework, or, at the least they motivate children to complete assignments. Should a child not complete his work, teachers should provide logical consequences at school. If a bad apple fails to handle this teaching responsibility, do not assume the burden yourself. Always separate your responsibility from the school's.

Guardians of the Grades

Grades are the nitroglycerin of the school system. An overemphasis on making good grades creates a Grade Trap which imprisons a child and destroys his innate striving for knowledge. Young children possess natural curiosity and a keen desire to learn about their world. An overemphasis on the importance of high grades exchanges the pursuit of learning for a pursuit of A's.

Getting stuck in the Grade Trap also diverts attention from the crucial personality traits that are developing during the school years. In the early school years, children learn to relate to others, to understand another's viewpoint, and to develop confidence in personal skills. An overemphasis on earning high grades may lead a child to believe self-worth depends solely upon academic achievement. Such a belief results in the creation of grade addicts and school losers. Ironically, because children divide the identity turf within a family, one child may become an addict while another feels like a failure.

High grade-point averages never predict personal

An overemphasis on the importance of high grades exchanges the pursuit of learning for a pursuit of A's.

happiness. In my career in the academic world, I meet Ph.D.s with glowing academic records who, nevertheless, lack the basic ability to relate well to others. An overemphasis on the academic world restricts their lives and the lives of their families and students. Somewhere early in life they fell into the Grade Trap and never escaped. Their lives lack balance.

One university I attended passed down a legend that warned students not to become unbalanced. The legend concerns a senior scholar who had a nearly perfect Graduate Record Exam score and a 4.0 grade point average. Already, a prestigious graduate school had accepted this student for study in the fall. But the day before a major senior's project was due, the young man partied too long. For the first time in his college career, he turned in a late paper, which resulted in his receiving a grade of B. On the day he earned his first grade lower than an A, the grade addict committed suicide. How unimportant grades appear when compared with the whole of life!

Many parents inadvertently stumble into the Grade Trap by using unwise techniques in motivating children. One common error is to "bribe for brains." Despite numerous studies warning that bribes backfire, parents still pay cash for A's, or make privileges contingent on improved grades.

A friend of mine plunged into the grade market by paying his daughter a dollar per A. Each grading period the dollar lost buying power and the daughter went on strike. After negotiating for higher pay, the daughter studied again. At last check, the going rate for an A was five dollars. And this child is still in elementary school!

Teachers also "bribe for brains" by awarding prizes to students who win academic contests. Of course, the students who are already doing well win the awards. For the highly motivated, rewards transform internal motivation into an external quest for tangible awards. Perfor-

One common error is to "bribe for brains."

mance declines in quality until the next academic sweepstakes begins. Ironically, academically impoverished students with little motivation to do well in school benefit most from gaining tangible rewards. But even with the intellectually delayed, rewards require extraordinary planning.

Pay in exchange for good grades simply does not benefit most children. As a mini-myth it feeds upon the host myth that parents are responsible for a child's education. Parents who become curators of A's throw children out of balance for a lifetime. Whether the young become grade addicts or feel like school losers, they fail to benefit from education.

> **Students with a passion for learning make good grades as a by-product of their work. For the addict, grades are their work.**

In college those caught in early grade traps reveal themselves quickly. Grade addicts rarely possess a passion to read and study on their own. Instead, they concentrate on the test material. Their most common questions are: "Will this be on the test?" and "Can I receive extra credit for reading this book?" Students with a passion for learning make good grades as a by-product of their work. For the addict, grades *are* their work.

Those captured in the Grade Trap "burn out" during the academic years. After graduation, many give up reading and learning, because tangible rewards for performance no longer follow. Victims of grade addiction soon become victims of repetition. You will find these former addicts sitting daily in front of televisions, or continuing their routine uninformed conversations with friends. Parents' enthusiasm for good grades robs many children of a quality education.

Distance Discipliner

Competent teachers inform parents about a child's serious misbehaviors but handle the problems in class. Less competent teachers request that parents make their child behave in the teacher's class. How ludicrous and unfair. Parents not present in a classroom can neither prevent nor discipline outbreaks of misbehavior. Classroom management must remain the teacher's job.

Skilled teachers establish rules and logical consequences understood by all students. Often, children enjoy being given a voice in creating the rules. Because good teachers systematically encourage positive behaviors, few students wander too far out of bounds. When exceptions occur, knowledgeable teachers calmly handle the problem themselves. Only the most extreme cases require administrative or parental involvement.

While most teachers discipline well, a few lack skills and common sense. Some make enemies among students by overreacting and dispensing harsh, illogical punishment. A few unskilled teachers humiliate students and increase the animosity between the student and teacher. Some berate children verbally. And still others continue irrational practices, such as requiring misbehaving students to copy pages from dictionaries and texts. Results are consistent. Small misbehaviors mushroom into school problems.

Permissive teachers also explode small misbehavior into catastrophic problems. Unable to establish and enforce logical rules and consequences, permissive teachers warn, yell, plead and, generally, attempt to whine problems away. Verbal attempts at discipline fail. Thus, the unskilled teacher seeks help from the outside. Principals and eventually parents become Distance Discipliners. Problems that actually began because of a teacher disability now create a new situation: a child with "school problems." Too many children become scapegoats for teacher inadequacy.

Here are accounts of why three families entered family counseling with a school-related problem. In one case, family counseling proved helpful, and in the other two the teacher needed training. In the first case, Rob

Problems that actually began because of a teacher disability now create a new situation: a child with "school problems."

and Linda Guthrie had considered divorce and this had created unbearable tension in the home. Their son Ronnie began to misbehave inside and outside of class. Whenever Ronnie misbehaved, Mr. and Mrs. Guthrie joined forces to face the problems he created. In Ronnie's private logic, his misbehavior seemed to bring unity to his parents. His teacher lacked power because of the family's dysfunctional system. During counseling, the Guthries became aware of the true nature of the problem and released Ronnie from his self-appointed role of marriage savior.

In the other cases, the families displayed positive family dynamics. Misbehavior isolated itself to an individual teacher's classroom. Tommy Patterson's family arrived in counseling with the apparent problem that their fourth-grader refused to do homework and repeatedly told his teacher that the work bored him. "The strange thing is," said the mother, "Tommy makes A's on all of the tests, but he receives D's on homework grades. We've yelled, reasoned, bribed and begged, but Tommy won't work at all. The teacher says we must see to it that he works at home. What's wrong with him?" In this case the problem was caused by an unimaginative, uninspiring teacher who failed to challenge and motivate her students. Instead, the teacher demanded obedience whether her homework proved helpful to students or not. The teacher created a power struggle and asked the family to join her side. The Pattersons paid a high price for the teacher's misbehavior.

Melissa Martin's kindergarten teacher announced to her parents that the child seemed hyperactive and possibly suffered from an Attention Deficit Disorder. "Melissa talks incessantly to friends and walks around the room without any regard for order," said the teacher, who suggested that the parents place the child on Ritalin and seek counseling. During our first one-hour session Melissa sat quietly in her chair and never acted inappropriately. The parents reported no unusual problems at home.

Why would Melissa exhibit two different sets of behaviors? Upon investigation, I discovered that the teacher presented immediate verbal attention to misbehaving children. She offered no behavioral consequences for misbehaviors and no encouragement for positive behaviors. At home and in my office, Melissa behaved because she received recognition for cooperation, not disruption. Because of the teacher's lack of discipline skills, Melissa earned attention the easy way, through misbehavior. Melissa was not hyperactive, but a lover of attention.

Although a few children present unmanageable problems for competent teachers, many others become the scapegoats of poor discipline systems. As an unfortunate child's misbehavior becomes an issue, the youngster earns the reputation of being a problem child. At worst, a victimized child may receive a label such as emotionally disturbed, a role which he may begin to accept and follow.

Unfortunately, many artificial disabilities arise because of poor classroom management. Otherwise assertive parents may become overly involved in the situation because they accept total responsibility for their child's success and failure in school. Parents' attempts to MAKE a child behave in school generally produce nothing but a negative home atmosphere. Therefore, support competent teachers. And remember: classroom discipline remains a teacher's job.

NEW AND IMPROVED BELIEF 8 YOU CAN LEAD A CHILD TO EDUCATION BUT YOU CAN'T MAKE HIM DRINK

Reinhold Niebuhr's sentiments provide the perfect guideline for school involvement. How nice it would be to MAKE our children drink from the

Grant us serenity to accept the things we cannot change; Courage to change the things we can, And wisdom to know the difference.. —Reinhold Niebuhr waters of education. But whenever parents become over-involved, attempting to force results, they wander into more complicated problems. When we try to control — rather than influence — another's life, our good intentions usually create more problems. So many factors influence school performance. Parents must discover the positive ways to encourage school success.

Homework: Opportunity and Modeling

By creating a schedule and proper atmosphere, parents encourage good study habits. Establishing a "quiet time" for homework and reading provides the foundations for study. Families need to agree on the hours for daily study. During the "quiet time," electronic media shuts down, and parents and children involve themselves in tasks such as reading or homework. Although the same time every day works best, often consistency becomes impossible because of a variety of commitments outside of the home; therefore, families need to establish their schedules together. Children should study at the same desk or table daily. Soon simply sitting at the desk triggers an expectation for work. Nothing substitutes for consistency and positive habits of study.

When a child observes a quiet time, parents must not use investigative activities, such as demanding to check homework or requiring the child to display completed work. Investigative parents will achieve only bad results from their good but overly demanding intentions. Help children only when they truly need it.

Good modeling remains the best method for influencing positive homework habits. Parents who take time to read and study raise children who believe that such qualities are a valuable part of living. On the other hand, parents who watch television frequently and avoid reading raise children who consider homework a punishment imposed by teachers. Never expect to raise a scholar from infertile academic soil.

Should teachers complain that your child neglects homework, check your contribution of the home essentials: a quiet time, a consistent place and modeling. Beef up any weak areas in home influence. Then ask the teacher for his plan to handle the challenge. A few teachers prefer that you solve their teaching problems. However, if you provide the home essentials, the teacher must do the rest.

Grades

Many parents neglect the importance of small decisions which have a significant impact on a child's performance. For example, the age of children when they enter school carries with it a significant influence on future grades and behavior. Males develop more slowly than females. When a male enters kindergarten as one of the youngest in the class, often it places him at a developmental disadvantage. Grades may suffer and behavior problems frequently result. If possible, delay a young male's entry into school.

Focus on the joy of learning, rather than on the grade. Responses such as "that really looks like fun," or "I am so pleased you enjoy math and English," build upon a child's natural drive to learn. Good grades generally follow as a consequence of parental enthusiasm. Comments such as "I am proud of your grades," or "I am so pleased to see an A in English and math," concentrate on the grade rather than the learning. Such an emphasis diverts a child from natural drives to learn to an unnatural pursuit of making good grades. As discussed above, those captured

Should teachers complain that your child neglects homework, check your contribution of the home essentials: a quiet time, a consistent place and modeling.

by the Grade Trap may become grade addicts or school losers.

When a child stumbles in a subject, dwell on the positive. Reinforce his interest in more successful areas and always leave open the possibility for change. A helpful response to report cards might be: "I am pleased you enjoy English so much. Who knows? Someday you may enjoy math just as much." The following response only discourages children: "You are great in English, but you always do poorly in math. You are just like your father." Avoid ALL comparisons of performance between siblings. Also bury your old war stories of personal success in school. Hearing stories about your past success usually discourages a child. A parent's influence rests in the ability to model enthusiasm for learning.

In the case of totally discouraged children, avoid all criticism. Consider seeing a family counselor who might offer suggestions for how best to encourage a child.

Discipline

Most teachers provide excellent discipline. But if your child misbehaves in one teacher's class and not in others, assume that a teacher problem may exist. Support both your child and the teacher's positive attempts to discipline.

Ask for a teacher-parent conference, but come prepared. Several basic questions should be asked: "What are your rules? Do your students know and understand them explicitly? What are your consequences for a child's breaking these rules? Do the children know which specific consequences will occur? What is your plan for encouraging my child?" If the teacher provides satisfactory responses to your questions, then support the teacher's plan. Avoid schemes that require double punishment — or punishment at school AND at home for the same

> A parent's influence rests in the ability to model enthusiasm for learning.

school offense. A teacher's classroom consequences should be strong enough to solve a student's misbehavior.

If the teacher appears unskilled, you might offer suggestions. Read books on classroom management. Texts can be located in *Books in Print* in your library. Also some systems of discipline prove successful such as Rudolph Dreikurs' *Maintaining Sanity in the Classroom,* Lee Cantor's *Assertive Discipline,* or William Glasser's *Schools Without Failure,* and *Control Theory in the Classroom* to mention a few.

Should conferences and communication fail, teach your child to play the system. Such a lesson in reality provides benefits for a lifetime. Instruct children that they must either follow the system's rules or display the courage to take the consequences. Then leave decisions and ensuing consequences to the child. Stand by your child's choices and encourage him. Remember: Control only what can be controlled.

> **Instruct children that they must either follow the system's rules or display the courage to take the consequences. Then leave decisions and ensuing consequences to the child.**

NEW PITFALL 8
TEACHERS ALWAYS
ARE AT FAULT

Our culture unjustly blames schools for many of its woes. Cases of teacher incompetence do exist. But often the origin of a child's school problems can be found in the family. School problems often occur when parents fail to provide the essential home conditions that foster good academic habits.

A rapidly growing problem in today's society revolves around the overcommitted parent. On the go all of the time, the overcommitted attend meetings, support organizations and endlessly participate in community activities. Children of the overcommitted seldom enjoy access to their parents. Good study habits fail to develop. Academic modeling rarely occurs, because no time is available for family reading or intellectual pursuits. Often, overinvolved parents expect school success from their children, but the seeds for this success remain unplanted.

Another group of families who are delinquent in planting proper seeds, also spawn the Street Corner Terrorists discussed earlier. These parents see little value in school and fail to encourage their children. Also, always on the go, academically impoverished parents rarely provide the essential home conditions necessary for success. Their children lack the motivation and modeling needed to develop adequate study habits. Because their family values exclude school success, academic prosperity rarely occurs. Unfortunately, under the present public school system, children of the academically impoverished rarely beat the odds.

As in the case of the Guthrie family, complicated family dynamics create school problems for children. Any major family tension, or any significant family change will overshadow the importance of school success in a child's life. Single parents and stepparents are keenly aware that their children need extra encouragement as they adapt to life changes. Until children find a positive, secure place in the family, they tend to be less concerned with school success. When a child's school problems continue for an unreasonable time, family counselors often can provide needed help.

In most cases, teachers motivate and discipline children well. Occasionally school problems occur because of the failure of an unskilled teacher or a poorly run school system, but school problems often begin at home. Parents need to check their home first, before casting blame on the schools.

Until children find a positive, secure place in the family, they tend to be less concerned with school success.

MYTH 9

"THERE WILL BE NO FIGHTING IN THIS HOUSE" Few recipes for failure create more distasteful results than the one forbidding sibling fights. Creating this self-defeating rule insures that parents will become overinvolved in the inevitable sibling rivalries of childhood. The "No Fighting" myth enters the Cookbook for Self-Defeat with other unsavory recipes, such as "I will NEVER break my diet again," or "I will NEVER lose my temper again." As with New Year's resolutions, if you must create a "No Fighting" rule, fine. But never take the rule seriously.

All healthy children enter into sibling rivalries. Inevitably, these rivalries lead to many forms of fighting. Some children verbally joust — through screams and whines — while others exchange shoves and an occasional punch, but many learn to manipulate their siblings through being charming or cunning. No matter what form the rivalry takes, such encounters appear as natural to childhood as sore throats and earaches.

Although most fighting appears to produce nothing positive, some skirmishes allow children to stand up for themselves and to negotiate with others. Children follow

> **All healthy children enter into sibling rivalries.**

Parents must establish a plan to handle fighting.

a natural developmental sequence thrusting them toward autonomy. The two-year-old resists invasions of his world by yelling, "No!" Ignoring the boundaries leads siblings into tough territorial fighting. Biting, hitting and yelling become weapons in the struggle for autonomy. Parents must establish a plan to handle fighting. But to enforce a prohibition of fighting risks creating a Fighting Rebel, resistant at every turn, or a Doormat Child, incapable of protecting personal territory.

A kindly doctor developed a staunch belief in passive resistance. Dr. Nelson insisted that his daughter, Mary, never fight for any reason. Although less convinced of the practicality of his stance, Mrs. Nelson also enforced the "No Fighting" policy. The parents failed to understand that children lack the intellectual skills to understand passive resistance. For a child, adherence to a "No Fighting" rule generally requires giving in to others' aggression and demands.

The Nelsons' policy interrupted the natural order of individual growth and sibling relationships. Mary attempted to please her parents by never fighting. As a result she never learned to stand up for herself or to say no to others. Mary Nelson, in a sense, became one of those Jello kids who rarely takes a firm stand. As an adult she still may fail to defend her own territory. A continuing discomfort in saying no to others may be the final result of her parents' passivity training.

Children learn to protect their interests early in life. Mrs. Johnson overprotected Sally, her eighteen-month-old. Whenever the Johnsons' four-year-old son, Joshua, picked on Sally, Mom charged to the rescue. As a consequence, Sally cried whenever Joshua approached. Sally's cries brought her safety in the arms of a protective mom. When the Johnsons realized that Sally needed to learn to defend herself, they decided to stay out of the children's fights.

Following a frustrating weaning period, Sally understood her cries would no longer bring instant help. Soon the parents observed Sally's first display of assertiveness. One evening Joshua stole a toy off of Sally's bed and turned to run past his helpless sister. Putting away her defenselessness, Sally raised her leg as the thief passed her. Wham! The oldest child fell to the floor in disbelief. Then Joshua jumped up and fled in tears to report the incident to his surprised parents.

As solutions to conflicts become more sophisticated, children cultivate new skills such as negotiation and salesmanship. In fact, sibling rivalry may be the spawning ground for lawyers and salesmen! Mark Twain's old story describing Tom Sawyer's feat in persuading his friends to whitewash the family's fence finds replication in a variety of sibling interactions.

For example, any family traveling in a normal-sized car with three children provides an institute for training real estate agents. Because no one wants the middle seat, each child tries to convince the other of its value. Those well-equipped at making an unfavorable piece of property sound appealing might convince a sibling to sit in the middle for the trip's duration — and enjoy every moment. Salesmanship grows from sibling rivalry.

Other children master the art of arbitration. In the example above, if no child succeeded in selling the middle seat, then an opportunity for arbitration arises. When I was young, my family often journeyed from Raleigh, North Carolina, to Lynchburg, Virginia, to visit grandparents. After preliminary bickering about seating accommodations had failed, my oldest sister would hammer out immaculate contracts. "You sit by the left window until we arrive in Roxboro, but you must surrender the seat when we reach the first stop light in South Boston. Then I move to the middle. . . ." And so it went. What started off as a fight led to the more advanced arts of compromising and influencing others through salesmanship, negotiation or logic. Such sibling exchanges commonly solve a variety of problems from use of the bathroom to music selection.

Occasionally, parents supportive of the "No Fighting" myth place children into impossible situations, which family therapists call a "double bind." Trapped in a no-win situation, children cannot find positive solutions. All options lead to defeat. The familiar son-in-law stories provide adult examples. A son-in-law disliked by his in-laws receives an invitation to bring his family to a Saturday lunch. The in-laws know Saturday is the young man's golf day. No matter what he decides, the son-in-law's Saturday is a lost cause. If he declines the invitation, his in-laws will be angry and his wife may be unhappy. But if he goes, his in-laws will find fault with all he does and he will miss his golf date. For him there exists no graceful exit.

Similarly, parents who on one hand teach children to "stand on their own two feet" and to "say what they really think and feel," may, on the other hand, punish children for sharing angry feelings and breaking the "No Fighting" rule. The Donaldson family provided a perfect example. Mr. Donaldson won decorations during his military service in Vietnam. When he returned to the United States, he experienced a religious conversion. Mr. Donaldson's military background influenced him to encourage his three sons to be tough and assertive. However, his new religious principles asserted that all fighting and anger is evil. These two opposing sets of rules confounded the Donaldson boys. Dad teased them when they appeared "soft" and scolded them when they fought. Frustration swelled. When left alone the Donaldson boys exploded at one another. Their fighting accelerated because of the presence of conflicting messages. Like Mr. Donaldson, many parents encourage children to be honest with their emotions, then punish them for sharing the WRONG emotions.

Poor parental legislation often increases the number

Many parents encourage children to be honest with their emotions, then punish them for sharing the WRONG emotions.

or intensity of fights. These mini-recipes for failure provide enough ingredients to insure daily frustration. For example, a common self-defeating rule requires toddlers to share their toys with others. Two-year-olds do not share well. Toys become a part of their territory which they resist surrendering. To force a toddler to share violates the child's growing sense of autonomy. Instead, parents can reduce fighting by removing the toy that has caused the fight. Most two-year-olds will find satisfaction in a compromise that prevents a rival taking possession of a loved object.

Many parents require that older children play with younger children "nicely." Such instructions create sticky problems for older children. The "Play Nicely" rule generally allows the youngest child free license to torment older siblings. Mr. and Mrs. Zigler raised two daughters, Martha, age thirteen, and Stacey, age three. Of course, the three-year-old preferred playing with Martha's possessions. The parents' "Play Nicely" rule soon allowed Stacey to become tyrannical. Stacey purposely frustrated Martha by disorganizing and misplacing Martha's most valued possessions. When Martha responded with anger, Stacey shrieked to Mom who then chastised Martha for not being more understanding and patient. Mrs. Zigler's intervention left Martha defenseless. Instead of allowing occasional territorial spats, the "Play Nicely" rule led Martha to nurture a hostility and resentment which found no outlet.

Children, like prize fighters, love spectators and referees. Rarely will young children fight without observers and judges. As soon as fights break out, youthful brawlers drift toward adult audiences. Parents too willingly accept the invitation to become Judge for a Day, and then through their involvement, become an integral part of the bouts.

Parents often make incompetent judges. When drawn into children's spats, parents commonly accuse the wrong

> The "Play Nicely" rule generally allows the youngest child free license to torment older siblings.

child of wrongdoing. The MacAbees' three children fought persistently during our initial counseling session. The script for the children's battles displayed the same predictability as those followed in professional wrestling. However, the parents remained oblivious to the repetitious episodes. Whenever the parents looked away, the youngest child, Tommy, taunted the middle child, Bryan. Resisting the temptation to skirmish, Bryan tried not to retaliate. But soon Tommy would push the right button. On one occasion Tommy licked his finger, then slyly rubbed it on Bryan's arm. Outraged, Bryan swatted Tommy. The swat and Tommy's yell gained the parent's attention.

Seeing only Bryan's offense, the parents yelled at the older child, threatening to enact severe reprisals at home. Weeping, Tommy appeared innocent and wronged. Instead of mounting a defense, Bryan stooped defiantly in his chair, guilty as charged. Bryan knew any pleas of innocence would elicit a "you-are-older-and-should-know-better" sermon. When fights occur, parents who allow themselves to be lured into the fray become an important part of the fighting. Parental overinvolvement increases their children's fighting.

Stepparents particularly must be careful when tempted to intervene in fights. In a sense, stepparents automatically inherit a "no-win" situation. Particularly if there are natural and stepchildren involved, stepparents will be accused of either showing favoritism to their natural children or of abandoning them. When it comes to fighting in a stepfamily, children must learn to solve their own skirmishes to become close. Constant intervention by adults keeps conflicts alive. Stepparents need to take a joint stand on how to handle fighting, or their homes may become a battleground.

No Recipe for Failure assures poorer results than "there will be no fighting in this house." Sibling rivalries result in occasional fracases. Although many skirmishes

Sibling rivalries result in occasional fracases. Although many skirmishes prove entirely useless, others help children reach important developmental objectives.

prove entirely useless, others help children reach important developmental objectives. "No fighting in this house" — no way!

NEW AND IMPROVED BELIEF 9
FIGHTING IS INEVITABLE, PLAN FOR IT.

Sibling rivalry and fighting remain natural parts of childhood. Instead of fighting against the current by declaring "No fighting," channel the waters toward productive ends. Parental energy directed toward formulating consistent plans for handling fighting earns rich rewards for individual children and the family as a whole. Family rules eventually reduce the number and intensity of fights.

RULE 1: Do Not Interfere in Fights

Children develop their own resources for settling fights. Parents who intervene to end fights practice peacemaking abilities, while children practice solely the skills of fighting. In fact, knowing that parents will apply the brakes allows siblings the freedom to step on the accelerator harder. By refusing to become involved, parents force children to develop their own peacemaking skills. Refuse to be manipulated and decline the invitation to become judge and jury. A wise parent's predictable response to fighting becomes, "I am sure you can handle it yourselves."

Not involving oneself in a child's fights shows respect for the child's ability to solve problems. For example, if two adults pressured you to enter their fight, your response might be; "Keep me out of this. This fight is between the two of you." Children deserve the same

A wise parent's predictable response to fighting becomes, "I am sure you can handle it yourselves."

respect. Being drawn into altercations creates more problems. Out of respect for yourself and your children, stay out of their fights and allow them to develop their own solutions.

In any neighborhood, a parent who needs to become the judge for children's brawls soon becomes overworked. Children bring their fights into the judge's yard, keeping the justice busy with a growing docket of trials. Small, emotionally charged lawyers plead their cases before the bench. In contrast, adults who refuse the status of judge enjoy relatively fight-free yards. As I heard one child advise two embattled newcomers to a friend's yard, "Oh, don't bother the Ellingwoods; they'll only say, 'Settle it yourselves.'"

Another variation on the non-interference rule is for parents to require children to take their fights outside or down to the basement. "You may fight, but not around us," parents declare. Almost never will deported fighters continue skirmishes. Children will fight at your inconvenience, but not theirs.

RULE 2: Hurters Need Time Out

Never listen to children's pleas of temporary insanity or diminished capacity.

"Anyone who hurts another person spends time in time-out." Time-out requires a child to spend time alone in an agreed upon place, such as a bedroom. Immediately the refrain begins: "But it wasn't my fault. She started it." Too bad. Hurters need time to regain self-control. Never listen to children's pleas of temporary insanity or diminished capacity. Teach children that they remain responsible for their behavior at all times, under all conditions. Sometimes accidental injuries do occur in fights. Nevertheless, the hurter participated in a situation that promoted the accident. Avoid the role of judge. Injuries are injuries. Help children prevent creating dangerous situations by enforcing a severity clause: "Hurters need time-out."

RULE 3: Discipline Co-Conspirators Equally

In most sibling fights, children work as a team. The old adage "it takes two to start a fight" describes the cooperation involved in children's altercations. Rudolf Dreikurs suggested that parents place all children "in the same boat" when misbehaviors that require collaboration occur. Although the best policy is that of staying out of fights, if parents *must* intervene, then to send all combatants to their rooms becomes the best policy. Although some parents prefer a judicial process that finds a single party guilty, children soon accept the "all in the same boat" policy. Children understand complicity.

Consistent enforcement of an "all in the same boat" rule reduces fighting. Children begin to monitor the rule themselves. For example, in our house children may bring their friends inside to play, until a fight erupts. With the first outbreak of fighting that requires adult intervention, all children must leave the house. By now the rule finds widespread acceptance. If two children begin to square off for verbal or physical battle, another child steps in, "Cut it out, you guys, or we'll all have to leave." Not wishing to accept the consequences for fighting and the disapproval of peers, the defused fighters turn their energies toward positive pursuits.

Some parents allow children a second chance. Although discipline that eliminates second-chance policies appears most effective, many parents prefer using an advance warning system. Two versions of second-chance policies include: "Yellow-light/Red-light" and "Strike Three; You're Out." In the first, parents say, "Yellow-light" to inform children that they are out of bounds and parental involvement nears. If fighting continues, parents

Most children allowed three strikes enjoy each opportunity!

say, "Red-light," indicating that children must accept an agreed-upon consequence — usually time-out in their room.

Even more relaxed justice occurs in the Three Strike Method. Parents say, "Strike one," on the first offense, "Strike two," on the second, and "Strike three," on the third. The third strike earns the agreed-upon consequence. Most children allowed three strikes enjoy each opportunity! More misbehavior occurs. Nevertheless, many parents prefer this more relaxed approach.

Parents who refuse to bow out of their children's fights may stay in the combat ring for life. As adults, children of overly involved parents still involve elders in their domestic and business quarrels. Between rounds, the aging fighters summon their parents' intervention. Never learning to solve their own disputes, these battling adults continue the family role: Children fight; parents solve fights.

Two grandparents entered counseling on their daughter's behalf. The Johnstones reported that their daughter, Sarah, fought frequently with her husband over her right to return to the workplace after the birth of their first child. I suggested that the Johnstones' daughter and husband should attend the counseling sessions because the problems involved them. The parents retorted: "Well, Sarah wanted us to come for her. She always follows our advice. It would be best for us to know your suggestions, so we can be sure Sarah follows directions correctly." The Johnstones felt needed because they solved their daughter's fights. Their intervention, however, prevented Sarah from developing basic problem-solving abilities. As a result, Sarah became dependent and helpless in situations that involved conflict.

Don't make children warriors. Create peacemakers by insisting that children settle their own fights.

**NEW PITFALL 9
NEVER INTERFERE
WITH FIGHTS**

Sometimes fighting goes beyond the boundaries of normal sibling rivalry. When fighting escalates in frequency and severity, despite proper interventions, assume that a child may be deeply discouraged. Counseling helps discouraged children find rewarding outlets for healthy expression.

In some families, one child may display repeated acts of violence. For instance, in the Haslam family the eldest son, Tommy, aged 13, became skilled in the martial arts. Tommy used his knowledge to attack and intimidate his younger brother and sister. Tommy's violence increased and injuries to siblings frequently occurred. Mr. Haslam avoided facing the seriousness of the situation with his misguided notion that "boys will be boys." Finally, after Tommy "accidentally" broke his brother's arm, Mrs. Haslam brought the children to counseling. Mr. Haslam refused to join them because he believed Tommy's behavior to be normal for a 13-year-old. When repeated acts of violence occur, children need help.

A few children establish a "tough guy" identity both in and out of the home. When children enjoy a reputation for intimidating and fighting with others, intervention helps. Sibling interactions should not imitate televised bouts of professional wrestling. When a child begins to accept the identity of a fighter, then he needs help. Take dangerous fighters out of the ring and put them into counseling. During extreme cases like these, parents must intervene in fights.

MYTH 10

SPORTS BUILD CHARACTER People, not sports, build character in children. The duty of teaching values and attitudes belongs to parents, grandparents and extended family. Sports simply provide a forum for displaying character. Coaches, teammates and others can add to a child's growing character, but sports are only games, capable of teaching no human values. They exert no more influence over character formation than other artistic expressions such as dance, music, opera, and theater. The arts join sports as mediums for expression. Because many can participate in athletics, sports provide a universal stage on which athletes perform.

Sports can magnify the best and worst in a person's character. If an athlete achieves fame, the magnification discloses the youth's character to a critical audience. If a young person has received proper training from his family — and later from coaches — spectators benefit from observing mature behavior from a gifted competitor. Most athletes, like most of the youth in society, display positive behavior. On the other hand, when an immature youth gains widespread recognition, observers often see

---

Sports can magnify the best and worst in a person's character.

foul displays of behavior both in competition and in the athlete's personal life. Sports do not create the positive or negative personality traits of an athlete, but they expose them.

A look at the national sports scene clearly shows that sports cannot build character. In our national evolution, sports have paraded to a position of unexpected prominence, a new "opiate for the masses." But soon fans discovered that the opium ran through the veins of too many of the gods of sport. When a few of the gods turned mortal, the dark side of sports exposed itself all too frequently.

High-level, competitive sports grew powerful with the help of a nationally held myth that winning is everything. Possibly a myth prompting the value of being first plays a significant role in our nation's strength. When critics attack the value of winning at all costs, cynics respond by reorganizing the myth: "Winning isn't everything, but it sure beats what's second best." Only a small step propels proponents of the victory mentality to the dangerous conclusion: People are winners or losers. No sympathy exists for "losers" on or off the playing fields.

Winners in sports often rise to stations once reserved for privileged classes. The public now realizes that the super athletes enjoy a caste with special privileges. Some colleges lower entrance requirements for athletes and shelter them from the rigors of learning. Many graduate without basic reading abilities or important business and social survival skills. These privileges eventually victimize athletes who may be unable to establish careers in professional sports, yet are unprepared for other professions.

The public now observes with disappointment a daily list of abuses as a few from the athletic caste display disdain for society's rules. Cases of plagiarism arise and college courts respond with a double standard. Some athletes on full scholarships (and headed for professional wealth) shoplift or commit more serious offenses. Non-athletes also violate the laws. But the difference is that often the courts slap the wrists of the high caste's members but fail to hold them accountable.

A few athletes who graduate into professional sports continue to display the best and worst of human values. There remain far more positive than negative models in sports. But our nation too often tolerates the bad actors on the national stage in both individual and team sports. New Ugly Americans rampage on international tennis courts, cursing linesmen and throwing obscene gestures toward paying customers. Children watch. Ice hockey earns the title "ice fighting." Clips of violence on ice appear in ads for the Stanley Cup finals hoping to attract viewers. Children watch. Yet many parents believe: Sports build character.

You can take an athlete away from his upbringing, but you cannot take past inluences away from the athlete.

Like other areas of life, sports undergo a kind of evolution. Maybe the days of pampered sports gods will pass and society will refuse to tolerate exhibitions of violence, drug use, greed and poor sportsmanship. But whether society controls some of these Sports Scoundrels or will be controlled by them remains undetermined. You can take an athlete away from his upbringing, but you cannot take past influences away from the athlete. The bad characters of sports create values in homes that too frequently have abandoned the child to the playground or have pampered the players.

Overwhelmed by their personal lives, some parents become unable or unwilling to teach and model values. Such adults sometimes abandon their children to neighborhood playgrounds. There, these Sports Orphans create their values alongside others who may share weak foundations. Occasionally, an adult outside of the family takes over a Sports Orphan and creates values and character not provided by parents, but such an adoption is rare.

Because parents often believe that sports build

character and dream of the success of the Athletic Caste, a few unwittingly make of sports a foster home. Assuming sports participation produces good sports under any conditions, some parents soon tend to ignore their responsibility to model and expect appropriate values, attitudes and behaviors. Their children are indentured to the world of sport.

Stories of such parents flow through the ranks of Little League baseball. While most parents behave normally, a few boo umpires and ridicule the children of opposing teams. They humiliate their own children who dare to fail. In one area where I lived, parental attendance was banned from summer games because of the irresponsible behavior of a handful of overzealous parents who actually began fistfights during the games of children!

Addiction to sports often comes when parental investment soars. If parents invest significant time, energy and money in a child's athletic career, they then expect returns. Some children never repay the debt and remain in athletics in hopes of striking it rich. That winning is everything becomes obvious to a child when the family celebrates victories and mourns defeats. Slaves of victory, these children feel driven to win.

A vivid memory of mine involves an incident which occurred during my summer as a touring tennis instructor in North Carolina. Traveling the state with players, I noticed that some parents attended every match, disputed each draw and coached passionately from the sidelines. Their children became either addicted to victory or terrified of defeat. One mother who seemed particularly overinvolved carried a bag labeled "Tennis Mother." Her daughter, and other children like her, grew to believe that self-esteem and love could be earned only by winning.

Coaches too can become enslaved by sports. Instead of helping to build character, a few become negative influences. Victory means recognition for the coach. To

> **If parents invest significant time, energy and money in a child's athletic career, they then expect returns.**

win, the better athletes play while less athletic children only observe. As a result, the less able children's confidence is exchanged for victory. What price should less skillful children pay to be on Peter Piper Packing Company's championship team?

One amusing incident I observed came when a misguided coach attempted to teach five-year-olds that winning is everything. The coach's T-ball baseball team lost a close game. Seizing the moment, the coach required his players to run laps as punishment. The irony of the situation became evident as the children ran with index fingers pointed, displaying the number one sign. The players thought they were victorious and considered their punishment to be a victory lap.

On another occasion, I observed a misplaced drill sergeant attempting to motivate children by yelling at them. A terrified seven-year-old came to the plate. Apparently he rarely made contact with the ball. His coach screamed for all to hear: "Relax and hit the damn ball this time. Don't strike out again!" The anxious child never moved the bat off his shoulder while striking out.

A few make it to professional ranks. A combination of generous innate ability, overriding self-discipline, and an inordinate number of good breaks can lead to pro careers. Experiencing all three ingredients is miraculous. Still, some addicts risk their youth to "make it big" rather than develop skills and values that are required for success in other areas of society. Narrow and treacherous is the bridge to stardom.

The Hall of Never Was and the Shrine of Almost Made It fills up daily with ex-players. Parents should look toward these ignoble fortresses of athletic dropouts before urging children toward their gates.

A revolution may take us away from the Professional Sports Age and to a Participant Sports Age. The days of pot-bellied, ex-athletes seems to be giving way to an age of activity. Aerobics, jogging, and lifelong sports prosper as leisure time increases. As years pass, our nation will develop a new set of sports beliefs. But parents cannot wait. Destroy one myth now: Sports do not build character.

Character is still built the old-fashioned way, by people. Parents forge the original values. Coaches may add to existing foundations.

**NEW AND IMPROVED BELIEF 10
SPORTS DO NOT BUILD
CHARACTER; PEOPLE DO**

Parents should ask themselves two important questions: *What do I want my child to learn from sports?* and *How should sports fit into my child's life?* Years ago, I read an article about a letter that Senator Bill Bradley's father allegedly wrote to his son. At the time, Bradley (a Rhodes Scholar and graduate of Princeton) was a professional basketball player for the New York Knicks. Unimpressed with the prominence of sports in his son's life, Bradley's dad was said to have asked his son, "When are you going to accomplish something worthwhile in your life?" Whether true or anecdotal, the story suggests that the proper place of sports in life should be well considered. For a few sports become a life calling. For the masses sports remain a pastime.

Whether pastime or profession, sports offer many opportunities to teach lessons and values. Children learn to expect and handle life's highs and lows by experiences in sports. Parents can demand an exhibition of good sportsmanship in both victory and defeat. The degree of self-discipline necessary for success in any area of life can be developed. Opportunities arise to teach respect for, and fair treatment of, those with less ability. Adults can

Character is still built the old-fashioned way, by people. Parents forge the original values. Coaches may add to existing foundations.

115

model a cooperation between and respect for those of different races and/or economic fortune.

In a drug-plagued culture, parents can encourage young athletes to develop positive physical attitudes that demand an abstinence from smoking and an avoidance of drugs. For many, sports participation can provide a partial identity which helps to establish security for a child through the adolescent years. Young people who experience difficult family changes may receive needed support from teams and coaches. To participate in sports that are supervised by caring adults prevents many young adults from looking for identity on the unsupervised streets of our cities. And for a fortunate few, sports may allow matriculation at a university and an education that would otherwise be unaffordable.

For families, sports can provide a timeless island that transcends the changing fads of new generations. Despite family transitions, the world of sports offers a link between generations. But parents must not guide a child to the playing fields with the false hope that sports will build character. That task continues to be the family's. Sports provide an opportunity for teaching and practicing family values. But the sports arena will not monitor itself. Take control. Ensure that the sports stage magnifies the qualities you teach your child.

Eventually parents may pass their children on to coaches who support and further the family's values. Any negative experiences young children have with coaches provide opportunities for parents to discuss family values and attitudes. But most coaches exert a positive influence by building on the family's teachings. Some even espouse values parents admire and fail to demonstrate themselves. In these cases, close, positive relationships develop between athletes and their coaching mentors.

Athletes engaged in college sports need people-coaches as well as athletic-coaches. People-coaches serve as guides for life by becoming involved with an athlete as

> **Sports participation can provide a partial identity which helps to establish security for a child through the adolescent years.**

a whole person. Instead of exploiting young men and women for their sports contributions, people-coaches lead them toward realistic, future goals.

At Wake Forest University, I was fortunate to participate in athletics under the care of a tennis coach, Jim Leighton. Although inducted to the Hall of Fame for his winning teams, his true accomplishments lay in his treatment of players. He practiced holistic coaching; he was a people-coach.

Early in my career I secretly held on to a childhood dream of one day playing at Wimbledon. But what Coach Leighton observed was a slow-footed player without power. One day, while we were driving back to the college campus from a match, Coach Leighton gently discussed my future in sports. He encouraged me to pursue graduate work and in a loving way set my life on a realistic course. Until that moment my hidden dreams had interfered with reasonable goal-setting. As kindly given as his advice was, it hurt me to face the end of my adolescent dream. It remains the kindest pain I have suffered.

As a holistic coach, Leighton supported players on every front. He pushed academics, helped students find needed summer jobs, and he shared our disappointing moments. Holistic coaches deserve a separate Hall of Fame. Fielding winning teams does not build character, but displaying love and concern for the whole athlete does.

As careers in sports end, what is most remembered are the people. Wins and losses merge together, but people remain as significant models. Each generation inherits legends and learns from the lives of contemporaries who model values important to their lives.

For my generation, legends existed of the courageous men who broke the color barrier, such as Jackie Robinson and Jesse Owens. The humor of Dizzy Dean and the flare for description of Casey Stengel enriched us. Wilma Rudolph displayed how to overcome adversity, and Althea

> **People-coaches serve as guides for life by becoming involved with an athlete as a whole person.**

Sports do not build character, but people with character often play and coach sports.

Gibson rose from the anonymity of New York City streets. Bill Bradley achieved excellence in the classroom, and Arthur Ashe modeled class around the globe.

Most athletes enjoy close friends who live by positive and healthy values. Sports do not build character, but people with character often play and coach sports. The sports world becomes the stage on which they can transmit important human values learned in the home.

NEW PITFALL 10
DON'T LET YOUR CHILDREN
GROW UP TO BE ATHLETES

Because of the abuses that abound in the "Sports Age of America," many detractors err by denouncing all sports and by discriminating against athletes. Such critics become blind to the positive contributions made by the majority of athletes participating in sports. For example, to many prejudiced professors and teachers, all athletes appear to be dim-witted students attempting to avoid responsibility by sliding through school on their athletic bellies. For those exhibiting extreme narrow-mindedness, athletes must prove their abilities and intelligence while others are assumed to be capable. This type of overreaction to the problem within the sports world breeds a new, deadly myth: Sports destroy character.

Likewise, some parents shun sports and encourage children to enter activities they consider to be more wholesome. This prejudice denies children the opportunity to develop skills and talents enjoyed by countless boys and girls. Often, sports-deprived children suffer the ridicule of peers who fail to understand why they cannot throw and catch. By pressuring their children into entering more protected areas of life, parents may present their children with an uphill struggle in being accepted.

In addition, they prohibit children from sharing the enjoyment inherent in healthy, athletic competition.

Like those who champion the belief that sports build positive character, those who crusade against athletic competition overestimate the influence of sports. People transmit values and standards. Sports simply provide a stage.

MYTH 11

"HE NEVER LISTENS UNTIL I START YELLING" Sometimes parents stumble onto the dangerous notion that they might be smarter than their children. Soon after making this error, another perilous idea follows: Maybe I can train my child never to misbehave.

The opposite of both of these delusions proves true. In their areas of expertise — such as misbehavior — children reign as supreme wizards. More important, children invest their skills and energy into the proper training of their parents. Young people discover early in their lives that parents vary in knowledge and skill in the art of raising children. Some parents require more training in this area than others do, but the young generally remain persistent and rarely give up on their parents' education. Also, some children discover that they must at times reeducate their parents. For example, children in single parent homes and stepfamilies notice that adults need retraining following major changes in family life.

How much energy children need to invest in tutoring their parents depends upon the satisfaction they find in their search for significance in the family. If parents properly encourage their children and help them feel like a needed part of the family, then young people direct their energies — for the most part — away from educating parents. Mind you, even happy children still misbehave, but only to keep their parents on their toes. After all, children don't want their parents to become too complacent.

Sometimes, however, parents appear to be undermotivated and begin to neglect their children's need for positive attention and encouragement. In such instances, the young must direct much of their energy toward training their wayward parents. Because parents resist training, mothers and fathers usually label their child's educational techniques as misbehavior. Children rarely are perturbed by this lack of appreciation for the tools of education and remain dedicated to their parents' rehabilitation.

Skillful children misbehave in a manner that indicates how their parents fail to live up to their natural abilities to raise children. For example, if parents decline to give encouragement to young people for their positive contributions and behaviors, their children respond with miserable behavior that forces their parents to give them attention for negative acts. The lesson is clear: I will gain your attention one way or the other. Wouldn't it be better to reinforce positive behaviors?

Disciplining parents in this symbolic way can become laborious when parents are slow to catch on. Many adults fail to understand that a child's misbehavior highlights an area of parental weakness. Some parents — those close to untrainable — continue to believe that children's misbehavior makes no sense at all. To them, each misbehavior represents a random, unintelligent challenge to parental authority. Such dull analyses by parents frustrate children. "Why can't parents work harder to catch on?" young people wonder.

> **Some parents — those close to untrainable — continue to believe that children's misbehavior makes no sense at all.**

A few stubborn parents resist learning, then escalate their parenting misbehaviors. In these cases children may resort to drastic teaching techniques.

Children pose riddles through misbehavior that they expect their parents to solve. Although this technique frustrates parents, it is good pedagogy not to provide the solutions to students' problems — no matter what their age. The following response by Mrs. Campbell appears to be one that is representative of the frustration experienced by many unenlightened parents: "My son Tom annoys and angers me constantly. You'd think he'd realize that he's driving me crazy!"

Of course Tom realizes this, for his teaching techniques are excellent. Unfortunately, his mother displays little talent for discovering the point of his repetitive lesson. His message is: You do not notice me when I behave well. Furthermore, you do not allow me any voice in family decisions. Therefore, I will make your life miserable too.

A few stubborn parents resist learning, then escalate their parenting misbehaviors. In these cases children may resort to drastic teaching techniques. Adults usually give derogatory names — such as delinquency or anorexia — to these educational tactics. When this type of severe training proves to be necessary, professionals often must help parents piece together the family puzzle.

A case in point is that of the Bedford family. The Bedfords each achieved professional success. Dr. Bedford's medical practice boomed and Mrs. Bedford became an outstanding corporate lawyer. They prized their marital relationship and spent time together to insure that it would flourish. Whenever one spouse left town to attend a convention or to present a paper, the other usually arranged to go along. When they traveled, which was often, they left their son Jimmy (age nine) with friends.

Jimmy felt neglected, so he decided to teach his parents a lesson. Whenever his mother and father left town, Jimmy created trouble. He would shoplift, break windows or engage in whatever activities were necessary to involve the legal authorities. But his parents proved hard to train. Jimmy's behaviors embarrassed them. Hurt, they responded — not by solving Jimmy's riddle — but by placing greater restrictions on him. Their anger made Jimmy feel more unloved; therefore, he created problems of more serious dimensions. A family counselor was called upon to help the Bedfords interpret their son's message. It was simple: Spend more time at home with me and give me the encouragement I need to feel loved. After the Bedfords gave Jimmy more time and encouragement, he dispensed with their training.

Children's training techniques generally carry four distinct messages that many experts call "goals." The first teaches: If you do not give me attention for being good, then I will demand it by being bad. The second message involves the use of power. The lesson states: If you are pushy, stubborn and overcontrolling, then I will be forced to show you who is the boss. The following account provides an example.

Mr. Alamance ruled with a heavy hand. Whenever Mark misbehaved, Mr. Alamance responded by yelling and giving him a whack on the rear. Finally, Mark tired of his father's misbehavior. On their next public outing, Mark misbehaved in order to lure his father into a power struggle. Easily seduced, Mr. Alamance responded predictably by spanking his son in front of a crowd. To show onlookers who was more powerful, Mark refused to cry. After Mr. Alamance failed this parenting exercise, Mark showed his total control of Dad by sticking out his tongue. Mr. Alamance felt humiliated and defeated. But future spankings indicated that Mr. Alamance had failed to learn more positive methods of intervention. Often it requires years for a child to train a bull-headed parent.

A third lesson that children offer pronounces: If you hurt me, I will hurt you worse. Mr. Wake often over-reacted to the snippy comments of his daughter, Sally. In one instance Sally angered him immediately before Mr.

> **Children's training techniques generally carry four distinct messages that many experts call "goals."**

Wake's boss joined the family for dinner. Mr. Wake spanked Sally and sent her to her room for an unreasonable length of time. Sally was hurt.

Later in the evening, Sally glared coldly at her father. Mr. Wake's embarrassment in the presence of his boss grew. Finally, he offered a minor reprimand to which she responded: "I hate you, Dad. You are always mean to me." Mr. Wake understood Sally's message: If you hurt me, I will hurt you worse.

The fourth message involves discouragement. When children believe they cannot succeed, they will refuse to work in the area of their discouragement. In such cases, children show their discouragement by discouraging their parents. By not trying to succeed, they send the obvious message: I give up. I cannot succeed. Leave me alone. In response, parents often throw their hands up and exclaim, "I've tried everything; I give up." Such reactions ignore the hidden message: Your techniques for motivating people have discouraged me.

Whenever children feel threats to their identity, their misbehavior escalates. For example, stepparents and single parents often see increased misbehavior immediately following a major change in the family. Smaller transitions also increase misbehavior. For example, beginning the school year, moving to a new location or adding a member to the family temporarily challenges children's identities. Until parents learn to help children discover secure identities or children work them out for themselves, the crisis continues.

Do you think that highly skilled parents who are adept in solving riddles raise children who behave perfectly? NEVER. Children enjoy the Sport of Misbehavior almost as much as the challenge of teaching their parents. Children frequently misbehave simply to keep their skills fine-tuned. After all, children can never tell when even the most sensitive and encouraging parents may backslide. In the event a parent becomes lazy, children must be ready to retrain him or her with the use of well-timed misbehaviors. Preschool children work daily on their artistry. Most parents observe with awe as preschool children run through their paces. Remember, it requires skill and timing for a two-year-old to bring his parents to their knees in a crisis. Children must be prepared.

"He never listens until I start yelling." Nonsense! He is just trying to tell his parents that they are never serious until they start screaming.

NEW AND IMPROVED BELIEF 11 CHILDREN'S MISBEHAVIOR ALWAYS HAS A GOAL Children prefer to find significance through their growing competencies and their positive behaviors. Responding quickly to encouragement, they enjoy learning to collaborate and cooperate with their parents. Certainly, children are not hostile hoodlums out "to get" parents, as some suggest. Nevertheless, all children misbehave. Some of their misbehavior is developmentally appropriate, as we have seen. Other misbehaviors occur in response to error in parenting. And still other misbehaviors arise as a result of a mood, or as was suggested above, for the daily sport of it. But no matter what the origin may be, there is help for parents in understanding the purpose of their children's misbehavior.

Alfred Adler and Rudolf Dreikurs described juvenile misbehaviors in terms of FOUR GOALS that children try to achieve: attention-getting, power, revenge, and assumed disability. Parents can understand most of a young child's misbehaviors by identifying which goal attracts the child. Adolescent misbehavior proves to be more difficult to analyze because peers become an additional influence on the teen's motives. Parents can learn to identify their

Failure to respond appropriately to misbehavior, as a rule, will increase the number of incidents and the severity of the misbehaviors.

children's goals because each goal elicits a different emotional reaction from within the parent: annoyance (from attention-getting), anger (from power), hurt (from revenge), and despair (from assumed disability).

The goals of a child's misbehavior may change from day to day. For example, a visit to a permissive relative or a night with too little sleep may temporarily increase and alter a child's misbehavior. But with time, the child will return to his normal misbehavior. Repeated use of one of the goals, however, may signal to a parent the need to analyze their parent-child relationship. Is there a message behind the consistent misbehavior? For example, is the parent being too indulgent? Is the child receiving enough encouragement for positive behaviors? Should the child be allowed more say in creating his own consequences?

Whether a message accompanies a child's consistent misbehavior or not, parents must respond to the misbehavior. Failure to respond appropriately to misbehavior, as a rule, will increase the number of incidents and the severity of the misbehaviors. Below is a description of each of the four goals and a few suggestions for handling each misbehavior.

GOAL 1: Attention-Getting

If you have ever tried to talk on the telephone with a preschool child nearby, chances are good that you understand attention-getting misbehaviors. Attention-getting misbehaviors occur when children demand attention, knowing that they should not. Usually these times occur when the parent is busy, working or talking with others. Children demand undue attention in a variety of ways, including cursing, fighting with siblings, dressing slowly, playing with their food, asking Why? repeatedly, requesting unneeded help, as well as by the invention of countless other attention-getting schemes.

At times, preschool children appear to have been trained by a horde of gnats. When frustrated parents feel like swatting their child out of the way, their annoyance demonstrates that the child's goal is attention-getting. To train a child seeking undue attention, remember never to give attention to inappropriate behaviors. First, ignore the attention-getting ploy. Then give your child attention based on your terms. For example, a child who is interrupting your conversation with a neighbor can be calmed by an unexpected, loving arm placed around his shoulder. However, parents need to maintain their conversation and avoid giving eye contact to the child.

If attention-getting misbehaviors continue, use logical and natural consequences to handle the situation. Also increase your use of encouragement to support your child's positive behaviors and contributions. Remember, when unsure how to respond to a child, always increase your use of encouragement — the miracle technique.

> **Remember, when unsure how to respond to a child, always increase your use of encouragement .**

GOAL 2: Power

Preschool children with expertise in knowing how to ignite power struggles display techniques similar to those of an underworld hit man. When they want their way they become tough, single-minded, and unrelenting. School-age children utilize, as a rule, the more sophisticated artistry typical of legal shysters who twist the facts around to support their viewpoints.

Whenever I teach college students about power struggles, I send them to local department stores to watch parents and children in the midst of confrontations. The following is a frequent scene in almost any store's toy department. A father tells his five-year-old son, "It's time for us to go." The five-year-old skillfully ignores his dad. Angry, Dad errs by escalating the conflict, "I said it's time to leave and I mean NOW!" The child again ignores his dad by using the famous Brer Rabbit technique. In response, his father, who is furious and humiliated, grabs his son's arm and pulls. His son falls to the floor and screams. Curious crowds gather to watch the outcome. Infuriated and desperate, Dad spanks his son, then drags him from the store. As their car leaves the parking lot, the father begins a lecture and his son knows that once again he has made Dad appear foolish.

In a power struggle, the adult says, "You are going to do what I want you to do when I want you to do it." The child responds, "No, I will do what I want to do when I want to do it." Neither side compromises. The major rule that governs power struggles is: Adults can never win.

Two-year-olds and teenagers possess the curious ability to lure parents into fights about absolutely nothing.

Children are willing to fight about anything. Their favorite fights involve eating, sleeping, toilet training, buying toys, cleaning bedrooms, lying, stealing, earning poor grades, using seat belts, doing homework and completing chores. Although these represent areas of expertise, remember that two-year-olds and teenagers possess the curious ability to lure parents into fights about absolutely nothing.

Stepfamilies face increased challenges in handling power struggles. Particularly in the first year or two in a stepfamily's life, children react stubbornly to their stepparent's authority. That's why adults in stepfamilies must create a united front. Nevertheless, because of power struggles, it's easier for the natural parent to discipline until the family identity settles.

The major rule for handling power struggles is: Avoid them. That's right. Adults cannot win a power struggle because children do not play by adult rules. They will yell, scream, kick and hit below the belt. Parents must either learn to avoid fights, or be prepared to suffer humiliation. Work with children to create logical consequences, then if children violate their end of the agreement, enact the consequences.

In the above example, the struggle could have been

avoided if the father had planned ahead: "Son, you may go shopping with me if you will agree to leave when I say we must. Is it a deal?" Most children will agree to fair terms in exchange for the opportunity to go to the store. Once it is time to leave the store, then the child may refuse to go. Now, it is time to train the child. A toddler may be given the choice of walking or of being carried from the building. If carried, a child's kicks and screams should not lure parents into talking or fighting. They should simply enact the agreed-upon consequence.

Older children learn faster by being "lost." For example if a child refuses to leave, the parents can walk toward the exit. Many adults actually leave the store, but because I have a cautious nature I prefer to watch a child from a distance. After a few moments pass, the child looks up, realizes he has been left, and panics. The "lost" child runs to the exit. I usually allow a few moments to pass to insure that the lesson becomes a memorable one, then I allow the child to find me as I walk out of the door. Rarely do children need retraining after they discover that parents intend to act and will not verbally or physically spar with them.

If parents find themselves involved in recurring power struggles, they should examine the parent-child relationship. Is there a lesson to be learned from the child's misbehavior? Is the child trying to show his parents that he feels powerless and he wants to have his opinions taken more seriously? If so, the parents might hold additional family meetings and allow the child a stronger voice in creating consequences. Children need to feel important. If parents make children feel powerless, then they demand power through rebellion. Not all power struggles carry a hidden message. At times, children fight simply to demand their own way. In either case, the rule remains the same: Never enter a power struggle.

GOAL 3: Revenge

Acts of revenge
always signal
a troubled
relationship
and must
be handled
with care.

When children feel hurt by their parents, they will discover a way to hurt their parents in return. Most parents have felt this hurt from time to time. Often a child's desire for revenge follows a lost power struggle. Statements such as, "Why can't you be nice like Tommy's dad?" or, to a stepparent, "You're not my real father!" are meant to strike at the heart.

Acts of revenge always signal a troubled relationship and must be handled with care. Attention-getting and power struggles are common to children in all families. But the goal of revenge should be seen rarely. When revenge is a child's goal, parents must not react to their own hurt by injuring the child further.

As a parent, you need to resist the temptation to say, for example, "I'm not as nice as Tommy's dad, because I don't have Tommy for a son." Instead, realize that your child feels hurt, whether or not the pain seems to you to be warranted. NEVER retaliate. ALWAYS encourage.

By understanding that the parent-child relationship is temporarily impaired, parents can begin the healing process. Often it helps to be alone with the child and to do fun things together. Withdraw all criticism, if possible. If revengeful behavior continues or escalates, professional help should be sought from a qualified family counselor. Often counselors can relieve the family's pain in a relatively short period of time.

GOAL 4: Assumed Disability

Severely discouraged children give up. They lose their self-confidence and attempt to retain their self-respect by not exposing their inadequacy. By not trying, they will no longer be forced to feel the humiliation that accompanies failing. If an assumed disability involves school work, professionals in the field of special education may be able to help. Many children with assumed disabilities are misdiagnosed as learning disabled — rather than motivationally disabled — and receive training from teachers in special education. Often, however, the area of a child's assumed disability occurs outside of school. Some avoid sports; others avoid work. Discouragement can strike in any area of life. When a child assumes a disability, it is always advisable to seek professional help.

Young children's misbehavior moves toward a goal. Because most misbehavior involves parents, adults can learn to quickly identify the goals and react appropriately. Then, instead of being controlled by their children, parents free themselves to react in ways that enrich family relationships.

When a child assumes a disability, it is always advisable to seek professional help.

NEW PITFALL 11
ALL MISBEHAVIOR IS
DIRECTED TOWARD PARENTS

Some Tom Sawyer exists in all of us. I bet that when you were a child you sneaked into the kitchen — against parental sanctions — and stole cookies or a piece of forbidden pie. Possibly you antagonized your brother or sister just because you enjoyed watching them react! And, no doubt, at least once you played hookey from school by feigning sickness or went swimming against the rules. In all of these cases, you probably wanted to AVOID parental detection.

Not all misbehavior that irks parents is directed toward them. Some is a product of their children's curiosity and initiative. Although disapproved of by parents, these behaviors rarely warrant strong parental concern. When parents err by believing that all misbehavior is an attempt to manipulate them, then they risk creating an adversarial relationship with children. True, most misbehaviors of young children may involve parents, but many times they do not. Children need to enjoy their own Tom Sawyer-style adventures. Once in a while, turn your eyes away and allow a child to sneak a little candy from the candy bowl.

MYTH 12

BAD CHILDREN LIE, CHEAT AND STEAL

Have you known adults who believe that only bad children lie, cheat and steal? They accept an old notion that "good" children should abide by adult moral standards and that any episode of lying, cheating or stealing forewarns parents that their young ruffian most likely will spend an eternity as a hoodlum. To old-school moralists, children appear to be either moral or immoral, either good or bad. A single violation of adult standards often provides sufficient evidence for condemnation. Such judgments wrongly place undue pressures on parents who take to heart the opinions of others.

New and improved Belief #12 suggests that children's misbehaviors are universal and, with proper handling, can even lead to positive gains in moral growth. Below is a typical case of childish illegalities. Analyze the case for a moment. Do you believe the elder in this account acted in the best interest of the child involved? Or do his actions reflect ideas that are sadly out of tune with the moral development of children?

Rev. Watkins was the minister of a mainline city church and his six-year-old son, James, had been caught

> To old-school moralists, children appear to be either moral or immoral, either good or bad.

133

by an elder stealing money from the collection plate. The elder, upset about the crime, began to interrogate others in the church about James' behaviors. Research unearthed new reports testifying to James' unethical activities.

Six weeks prior to the theft, James' Sunday School teacher discovered him cheating during a game of Bible trivia. The youth group sponsor reported that several months ago James lost his temper and knocked to the floor a child half his size. Disturbed by these revelations of James' devilish behaviors, the elder presented his research to Rev. Watkins. "We are concerned about the path your son has taken," confided the elder. "I hope you will intervene before it becomes too late to help him. Something has gone wrong." Rev. Watkins replied: "I am stunned. He seems to be like the other kids. My wife and I have been very careful to train him well."

What do you think? Are the elder's actions justified and will they prove helpful to James? The picture painted by the elder depicts the youngster as a fiendish child, who — without immediate intervention — may be doomed to an adolescence and adulthood of delinquency and worse.

True, the elder's concern for James is sincere. He believes in the all-or-nothing view that morality — like inheritance — is something "you either have or you don't." To the elder, it seems that the child clearly lacks morality and the father must change his child-raising strategies to force the misdirected child back onto the proper course. With feedback such as the elder's, Rev. Watkins found himself in a parenting crisis. How much should the opinions of others influence a parent's child-raising strategies? Should he be alarmed? Should he quickly change his tactics? Will James be destined to a life of heinous crime if the elder's advice is ignored?

New beliefs support neither the elder's interpretation of the six-year-old's behavior nor the advice he offered the father. Instead, they suggest that growth in moral thinking is a lifelong journey. Parents serve as major guides for the wayfarer. Children frequently err in the early years of travel, but parents should not overreact. The development of more sophisticated moral thought requires proper training, experience and TIME. The road to growth in moral thinking passes through several significant check points that developmentalists call stages. Some of the territory between stages is filled with rough ground and hazardous conditions. During the early periods of travel, ALL children will occasionally lie, cheat and steal. Parents need to respond by applying the appropriate training techniques used for other indiscretions. Fortunately, most children are not observed by outsiders as closely as this minister's child was; therefore, they escape the stigma often caused by concerned but misguided adults.

Many older adults — who no longer raise young children — may counter: "When I was a child, I never lied, cheated or stole anything. In fact, I don't recall that any of my children did either." Preposterous! Such statements are an indication of a human condition called Post-Parenting Amnesia. Symptoms of this disorder include a total lack of recall of unflattering memories and the desire to appear superior to others based on unsubstantiated past performances. The effect on young parents of these claims of perfect moral behavior always is the same: GUILT.

Here's a true-false test. "Bad" adults — on occasion — lied, cheated, and stole when they were children. True. "Good" adults — on occasion — lied, cheated, and stole when they were children. True. Parents are powerless in guiding their children to enriched stages of moral thinking. False.

ALL children will occasionally lie, cheat and steal.

**NEW AND IMPROVED BELIEF 12
RELAX, CHILDREN'S
MORALITY DEVELOPS
SLOWLY — THROUGH STAGES**

Can a child who is a scalawag at age six eventually become a supreme court justice? Certainly! All children go through stages when their moral decisions are based on self-centered considerations. During these early stages, misbehaviors — such as lying, cheating and stealing — predictably occur. But by properly handling such incidents, parents enable their children to move to new, less selfish stages of thought.

One of the educators responsible for relieving many of the unrealistic fears of parents was Lawrence Kohlberg of Harvard University. Of Kohlberg's six stages of moral thought, the first four include all young children and teens.

Because of cognitive limitations, not all people can journey to higher stages. For example, severely retarded adults may not be capable of passing the first two stages. However, most children who are properly trained and disciplined will move into the third or fourth stages sometime during adolescence. A few, as adults, will receive the moral training and experiences necessary to continue their growth to higher stages.

Parents play a major role in nurturing their children's moral thought. For moral growth to occur, children need to experience positive conflict. By presenting their children with moral decisions and dilemmas and then displaying respect by listening to their opinions, parents place children in learning situations. After children express their views, parents then may suggest alternatives that the youngsters did not consider. Parents need to insure that their moral reasoning stays within a child's grasp, because children can understand moral thinking only one stage ahead of their own.

> **All children go through stages when their moral decisions are based on self-centered considerations. During these early stages, misbehaviors — such as lying, cheating and stealing — predictably occur.**

Although the situations that arise in daily life usually provide the opportunities to practice moral reasoning, some parents draw upon experiences from outside of family life. For example, in a few families a parent reads aloud the letters written to Ann Landers or Abigail Van Buren and then gives every family member the opportunity to suggest replies. Children enjoy the opportunity to be heard and to hear a variety of solutions to a single moral dilemma.

Parental modeling provides an example of the moral courage that children will need to enable them to act in ways that support their beliefs. For example, if parents ridicule a racial or ethnic minority after teaching their children the ideal that all people deserve to be treated with respect, then their children learn that ideals need not be carefully followed. On the other hand, when parents live by their ideals, despite criticism from others, they model the principle that those ideals can guide behavior even in difficult situations.

Adults in single parent homes and stepfamilies find their life situations to be fertile ground for teaching morality and for modeling. So many complex dynamics among people exist in non-traditional families that children often learn how to treat others despite their emotional desire to do the opposite. Respect for others and fair play in difficult situations becomes the family's norm. In the future, I suspect some of our finest moral thinkers will grow from the rich soil inherent in the life of non-traditional families.

Methods of parental discipline are a crucial influence on the growth of moral thought. Permissive parents fail to hold children accountable for their moral decisions. In addition, permissive parents generally provide a poor model for moral courage because they fail to back up their words with actions. Authoritarian parents may enjoy more success with children still in the lowest stage of moral thought because they generally act as they believe. But

Permissive parents generally provide a poor model for moral courage because they fail to back up their words with actions.

their methods may deny their children the necessary involvement with moral decisions and reasoning required for growth in moral thinking. Authoritarian parents generally dictate morality, rather than discuss it. Logical and natural consequences, along with good communication techniques, prove to be more effective in enhancing morality at every level. Parents who involve their children in the discipline process, as well as openly discuss options for solving moral dilemmas, provide the positive conflict necessary for continuing moral growth.

Kohlberg's three periods of moral thought include the Pre-Conventional Period (Stages 1 and 2), the Conventional Period (Stages 3 and 4), and the Post-Conventional Period (Stages 5, and 6). Children age ten and under display pre-conventional thought and adolescents generally move toward conventional thinking. In later adulthood, a few well-trained individuals may journey toward post-conventional thought.

Because no stage can be skipped along the way, we can be assured that each of us acted like a scalawag at one time or another.

Pre-Conventional Period

Parents should not be overly concerned about their children's self-centered thought.

Although children often delight their parents with an occasionally profound moral thought, young people, age ten and under, predominantly think in pre-conventional terms. In these first two stages, children are egocentric. Morality depends upon their efforts to avoid punishment or upon their changing desires. Parents should not be overly concerned about their children's self-centered thought. By teaching children family values and by exposing them to others' ideas, parents direct their children toward conventional moral thinking. Children generally move to the second stage during preschool years and to conventional thought during the late elementary or middle school years.

STAGE 1: No!

To toddlers the word "no" signals trouble. In these years, children obey because they wish to avoid the displeasure of authority figures, as well as the consequences that they might impose. Although children may not understand why a stove or stairwell offers danger, they know that their parents will not tolerate their experimentation with them. What directs a child's behavior is not an internal code of ethics, but a respect for and a fear of the power of those in control.

Adults from time to time overhear peers make decisions that are based on fear, rather than moral principles. For example, an adult might say, "I would never cheat on my income tax because I'm sure I would be caught." Such thinking does not consider the morality of cheating, but is concerned simply with the desire to avoid future negative consequences.

Similarly, if you ask a school child, "Why should you behave when your teacher leaves the class?," you might hear a reply representative of Stage 1, "Because the teacher might peek through the window and catch you," or "Because someone might tell on you and get you in trouble."

To discipline Stage 1 thinkers effectively, parents need to say no and then, if necessary, enact appropriate consequences that offer legitimate choices. For example, the use of time-out forces a child to make an important decision: I can stay here and behave, or I can misbehave and go to my room. This early emphasis on holding children accountable for their decisions teaches children to be responsible for their thinking. Permissiveness fails to enhance moral growth because children soon learn that

Permissiveness fails to enhance moral growth because children soon learn that parents may warn, plead and yell, but they will not act.

parents may warn, plead and yell, but they will not act. Childrens' decisions become inconsequential because all power rests in their hands. Authoritarians find some success in parenting toddlers. But soon toddlers, who do fear punishment, move to Stage 2 where they will attempt to avoid punishment in any possible way. Ironically, authoritarian parents create conditions that foster lying and sneaky misbehavior, or force a complacency based on fear of parental displeasure and/or punishment.

STAGE 2: Scratch My Back and I'll Scratch Yours

"I want what I want when I want it" appears to be the theme of Stage 2 moral thought. To use methods such as lying, cheating, and stealing seems acceptable as long as their use allows children to get what they want and insures that their actions will go undetected. For example, children may sneak forbidden change from their dad's trousers, break a household item and hide its broken parts, cheat in family games, or lie to avoid punishment.

One curious feature of thinking in Stage 2 is the lack of guilt present. Because children's (or adults') actions display the intense self-centeredness characteristic of this stage, they appear to be centered only on what is advantageous to them. Consequently, they worry little about the correctness of their behaviors, or about how their actions may affect others. If caught in crime, Stage 2 thinkers usually feel anger toward those who caught them rather than repentance because of their own behavior.

Stage 2 thought is not unknown to adults. Many adults never graduate from self-centered thinking. They attempt to take whatever they want through lying, cheating, stealing, or even force. Afterward, no guilt emerges. Criminals, whether prosecuted or undetected, often are guided by Stage 2 thought. Also, from time to time, the majority of adults generate random Stage 2 thoughts, such as, I'll bet that if I never report this extra income the I.R.S. will never find out. Most adults avoid the temptation to follow their Stage 2 thoughts and prefer instead to follow the dictates of their more disciplined moral thinking.

Children in Stage 2 enjoy learning to make trade-offs. Contingencies, such as, "When you finish clearing off the supper table, then we will play baseball," work well with Stage 2 thinkers. Family councils allow children to practice making deals and contingencies. For example, "If you dry the dishes and vacuum the den, then I will have time to take you to the store on Wednesday." Children slowly learn that their positive behaviors bring more rewards than their negative actions. Soon they increase their positive behaviors partly because they find it more beneficial to behave well.

If asked, "Why should you behave when your teacher is out of the room?" responses may range from, "You don't have to behave, if you post a lookout at the door to warn everyone when the teacher is returning," to, "Because if we behave well, she will allow us ten extra minutes for recess."

Teachers and parents should not be surprised to find a child occasionally cheating, stealing, or lying. These behaviors do not appear to be major violations in a young child's mind. By using appropriate consequences, parents can teach children that these violations will not bring them as much happiness and satisfaction as their positive actions can bring. Later, when in Stage 3, children will accept their parents' message that good boys and girls "don't lie, cheat or steal."

Logical and natural consequences work well with the self-centered thought reflected in Stage 2 morality. Stolen property must be returned to owners and broken items replaced by allowance money. Children are, therefore, required to experience the consequences of their choices, rather than to receive punishment that is non-educational.

Authoritarian parents tend to create an atmosphere of fear and anxiety that increases a child's tendency to lie to avoid stern punishment. Children lie, not because they are bad, but because they fear to tell the truth. If authoritarian techniques are combined with a general hostility and coldness toward children, then youngsters may enter the world of juvenile delinquency. Permissiveness provides equally poor results. When parents provide no limits, they create the Street Corner Terrorists and Monsters of the Classroom described in Myth #6.

Stage 2 thinking particularly worries parents. Children — on their worst days — seem destined to be hooligans and hoodlums for life. But such worries are unfounded. Parents who communicate well and use appropriate consequences can be confident that their children will soon adopt family values and begin to consider the feelings and thoughts of others.

> **Children lie, not because they are bad, but because they fear to tell the truth.**

Conventional Period: STAGES 3 and 4

Most adolescents journey to stages that reflect conventional moral thought. There they accept many of the values of their family and friends. Being less self-centered, those who exhibit conventional moral thought consider how their behaviors influence and are accepted by others. Conflicting loyalties may ignite internal conflicts. Also adolescents now face the lifelong challenge to act in ways that are consistent with their moral thought.

STAGE 3: Good Boys and Girls

A tremendous advancement in moral thought occurs when children move from a "what's in it for ME?" stance to a desire to be thought of as a "good" person in the eyes of OTHERS. Relationships increase in importance as Stage 3 thinkers worry about how others might perceive their behaviors. Family beliefs and values set a standard against which the values of other groups are measured. Young people who enjoy good relationships with their parents generally choose to support groups whose values are similar to those of their families. For example, teenagers might say, "We are students at Eleanor Roosevelt Junior High School and we are the best because. . ." or, "We are Americans and we believe in freedom and. . ."

Parents now enjoy the fruits of their repeated interventions that stressed family values, such as, "I don't care what other children do, you are a McHenry and the McHenrys don't do that because. . ." Parents find some relief from those days in early childhood when children misbehaved with apparent regularity. But in its place many worry—often unnecessarily—about the influence of peer groups on their children. By and large adolescents accept parental values and monitor their own behavior well.

The research of Carol Gilligan, an associate of Kohlberg's, implies that the priority on human relationships created by Stage 3 thinking may become the key to the world's survival. When people extend their family to include the world community, then the chance of nuclear destruction may decrease. The value of Stage 3 moral thinking may be underestimated. After all, positive relationships — not the law, strength or intimidation —may eventually save our world. Whether or not Stage 3 should be placed higher in Kohlberg's scheme is a debate that will continue.

Every stage of moral thinking encounters its own conflicts. Those who value the ideals of their family and associates must decide how to treat outsiders who hold different values. Also stressful are those situations when one's personal beliefs collide with those of others whose

Positive relationships— not the law, strength or intimidation —may eventually save our world.

opinions are valued. Stepfamilies often see their children struggle with the problem of how a good child should show loyalty to natural parents. Sometimes they feel disloyal when they obey their stepparents or even when they feel positively toward them. Adults need to be patient as children learn to respond to situations that elicit conflicting loyalties. For example, teenagers may experience anxiety when a peer group demands behaviors that are at odds with accepted family values.

A Stage 3 person may violate laws or norms if those significant to him approve. For example, an adult might say: "This tax law is unfair. Everyone I know refuses to report income they earn for work done on a private job. I'm certainly not going to be the only one to pay taxes on extra efforts." Similarly, a student might respond to the question, "Why should one behave when the teacher is out of the room?" with answers such as, "She trusts us and we like her; so we always do what she asks," or, "She is really a jerk, no one does what she asks." A typical response that irritates many parents begins, "Well, everyone else is doing it, besides. . ."

Parental techniques for teaching alternative solutions to moral dilemmas continue to benefit children. Family councils provide a forum for practicing cooperation and expressing opinions. On the other hand, permissive parents who abandon their children to the clutches of peer groups may surrender their influence. Also parents who continue to practice authoritarian techniques breed discontent and rebellion. A generation gap quickly spreads and a stormy adolescence may take place.

> **Permissive parents who abandon their children to the clutches of peer groups may surrender their influence.**

STAGE 4: Law and Order

In their mid-teens a few children enter Stage 4: Law and Order. They believe their duty requires them to follow the laws of their family, school, or nation. Loyalty to one's duty and the law is given even when the rules are disagreeable. Although many teens do not enter this stage, most who do are trustworthy and self-managing.

A Stage 4 thinker's response to tax-related questions might take on the traditional preface: "What if everyone in the world decided not to pay taxes because they disliked the laws or could avoid detection?" Students might respond to the question of how they should behave in the teacher's absence with responses such as: "We should behave well because we told her we would. Besides if everyone misbehaved, we couldn't complete our work. We are here to learn."

Problems may originate for Stage 4 thinkers when exceptions to rules appear warranted. But often exceptions are not made. Probably most readers have experienced the frustration of encountering a person who wishes to enforce a law that makes absolutely no sense in the given situation. But a Stage 4 response to the dilemma emphasizes that a "rule is a rule."

Communications between parents and their children continue to be important. Obviously, this is an easy period to create mutually made rules and consequences. Stage 4 thinkers monitor themselves well and they generally are willing to take the consequences of their behavior. In some cases, conflicts can now arise when adolescents' moral thinking exceeds that of their parents or teachers!

Now, let's return to Rev. Watkins' confrontation with the elder. Do you believe that James is a child on the path to moral destruction? Not according to the new and improved belief. Instead, James is a child on his way to Stage 3 in moral thinking. As long as the elders don't convince James that he is a "bad child" destined to a lifetime of fiendish behavior, he should progress well. If Rev. Watkins continues to provide the proper conflict, education and modeling, James may eventually possess the true wisdom of an elder. Before long Rev. Watkins' unenlightened elder will become astonished at how well "James Watkins turned out."

Kohlberg's stages describe moral THOUGHT but do not predict the growth of moral courage.

NEW PITFALL 12
HIGHER MORAL STAGES ALWAYS LEAD TO MORAL BEHAVIOR

Humans do not always possess the moral courage required to act in ways that support their beliefs. Kohlberg's stages describe moral THOUGHT but do not predict the growth of moral courage. Advanced thought does allow young people to consider how people SHOULD behave. That's important, because a person must be able to think of a response before he can act in that way. But actions often fall short of ideals.

For example, very few drivers can claim that they have come to a complete stop at every stop sign or that they stopped each time before turning "right on red." Did these drivers know right from wrong at those moments? Ask them whether or not their driving would have been the same if a policeman had been at the intersection! Chances are they willfully broke the law, although they "knew better."

Probably the most important factor in determining whether or not a child will display moral courage involves parental modeling. Parents who act in accord with their beliefs set a powerful example for their children. It is not enough to place a child in moral conflict, to provide responses different from his own, and to parent with the use of positive techniques. To raise a child who displays moral courage, parents must model that courage themselves. Parents whose actions support their beliefs follow good advice from the past: PRACTICE WHAT YOU PREACH.

MYTH 13

RAISING CHILDREN IS A SERIOUS BUSINESS

WHEREAS parents try to provide encouragement, avoid negative criticism., take time for training, arrange logical and natural consequences, shun permissive techniques, employ time out, reinforce positive behaviors, cultivate good communication skills, bypass authoritarian practices, share feelings, practice the use of "I" statements, set limits, build structure, and teach positive dental hygiene. . .

WHEREAS parents are charged by experts to analyze the goals of children's misbehavior, be appreciative of their stage of morality, ignore fighting, control the challenge of television, be aware of the importance of the first six years of life, be conscious of children's cognitive limitations, manage sibling rivalry, respond to school problems, supervise chores, create positive attitudes in sports, hold family meetings, walk away from temper tantrums, expect age-appropriate misbehaviors and look at filthy bedrooms. . .

WHEREAS parents, at the same time they are raising children, must develop their own abilities and provide well for their families while being challenged to enrich marriages, adjust to divorce, blend stepfamilies, arrange appropriate daycare, juggle dual-career schedules, pay off mortgages, wash and dry the laundry, pay monthly bills, clean their homes, survive taxes, face audits, avert burn-out, face the threat of unemployment, donate their "fair share," care for aging parents, invest for retirement, follow religious beliefs, accept the reality of death, stop smoking, observe diets, exercise regularly and remember yearly car inspections. . .

WHEREAS all of these things must be done in a world facing the threats of terrorism, nuclear destruction, cold wars, hot wars, revolutions, Third World dissatisfaction, racial inequality, assassinations, hostile ideologies, hostage situations, droughts, famine, poverty, starvation, overpopulation, street crime, drug cultures and the boycotting of international sports events. . .

THEREBY PARENTS DECLARE THAT: RAISING CHILDREN IS A SERIOUS MATTER; HOWEVER THAT:

SOMEDAY they will enjoy their children more,
SOMEDAY they will take more time to play
      with their children,
SOMEDAY they will recapture their
      own spirit of childhood,
SOMEDAY everyone will be happy, and
TO THIS END, every family has a plan.

The Family Vacation

Most goal-oriented parents prefer to schedule a family vacation. During this week or two, all family members are expected to enjoy enough family fun to satisfy them for a year. Occasionally, Vacation Families will be seen having fun at other designated times of the year, such as Christmas or Thanksgiving. But their true quest for happiness begins when the family packs, travels a distance, and directs itself "to have nothing but fun for a week." Now you and I know how family vacations go.

On the first day, parents rejoice upon reaching their destination, enjoy the rigors of unpacking, but soon discover they have nothing to do. Bored silly — but not wanting to admit it — parents pace up and down, rearrange the kitchen supplies and then down a stiff drink "to celebrate." As the hours pass, adults begin to reassure themselves that they are having fun by saying trite things, such as "This is the life." "Isn't this the greatest?" "I could do this forever." But in truth, they don't do it well for a single day. For months, most have not practiced the enjoyment of living together.

But never fear, parental ingenuity comes to the rescue overnight, and the next morning the parent who requires more structure unveils: The Schedule. "Tomorrow morning we will fish from 6 a.m. to 8 a.m. Swimming will begin at 9 a.m. and conclude at 11 a.m. Don't forget to put on your #15 suntan lotion. Lunch will begin at noon, then clean-up follows immediately. There will be a rest period from 1:30 to 2:30; then prepare for the water-slides." And so it goes. Everyone is back on a schedule! Now, the kids can return to fighting and irritated parents can resume yelling. But most important, everyone is WORKING HARD AT HAVING FUN.

> Fun always lies just down the road; happiness lurks around the corner.

The Future Train

Somewhere many parents hopped aboard a train bound to future happiness. For them, fun always lies just down the road; happiness lurks around the corner. In the interim, many families don't seem to enjoy living together too much or too often. For the past decade, I have asked parents attending our parent-study program: "What do you do as a family to have fun?" The question almost

Raising children is a serious business! True, for those who have forgotten that HAPPINESS IS A WAY OF LIFE.

always is followed by a somber silence. Then parents begin to explain why they never have the time to have fun together.

Similarly, I discover that many joyless families attend counseling sessions with the hope of discovering a miraculous communication technique or of learning an ingenious discipline ploy that will "turn the family around." Often, these families do not suffer from mechanical disabilities. They simply don't know how to enjoy family living.

Often the Overcommitted are the ones who left family happiness behind when they boarded a train to future happiness that has no stops along the way. Where did they join the train? Who knows? But all boarders handed the conductor a book of tickets marked: WAIT UNTILS.

Wait Until I get out of college and into
        the real world, then I will be happy.
Wait Until I find the right person to marry, then . . .
Wait Until I find the right house, then . . .
Wait Until I pay off the mortgage in 35 years, then . . .
Wait Until we have children, then . . .
Wait Until all of my children are out of diapers, then . . .
Wait Until my youngest child enters school, then . . .
Wait Until I no longer have a teenager, then . . .
Wait Until I send my last child to college, then . . .
Wait Until my youngest child graduates
        from college, then . . .
Wait Until I save enough money to retire, then . . .

At the end of the train's journey, parents begin the "I WISHES." "Now that I have the time and money to enjoy life, I just don't have the health and energy. . . . I WISH . . ."

Raising children is a serious business! True, *for those who have forgotten that HAPPINESS IS A WAY OF LIFE.*

**NEW AND IMPROVED BELIEF 13
HAPPINESS IS A WAY OF LIFE**

Dreams of future happiness lure many mothers and fathers away from the daily joys of family living. But some parents decide that they no longer can allow their days to slide by. Yet, removed from the habit of traveling through life happily, they often are unsure how to enjoy living in the present. Fortunately, for those whose skills for living happily have grown rusty, there may be expert teachers in the home.

Preschoolers live for the moment. For example, watch a group of four-year-olds at play. For hours, their happiness abounds as they give the gift of speech to favorite dolls; create adventures in the rugged living room terrain; ride their tricycles tirelessly on the sidewalk; and talk intently to themselves, just for the sake of a good conversation. How they enjoy this gift of living.

Adults often lose perspective if their emphasis is placed solely on future happiness. They plan for happiness as a coming event: a camping trip, a week at the beach, a ride through the mountains, a trip to an entertainment center, or a visit to their relatives' homes. These experiences provide children with life-long memories; such occasions enrich the lives of each family member, and offer children a sense of family togetherness, but what is *lost in the balance* is the daily happiness family life affords.

Seriousness in many families overwhelms any possibility for joy. Adults who face difficult life challenges may become too wrapped up in their personal problems to enjoy the opportunities for family frolic. For example, adults in single parent homes and stepfamilies may face added worries that lend an air of seriousness to the family atmosphere. Often, adults wait to be happy until something miraculous happens to make life "settle down" or to

> Seriousness in many families overwhelms any possibility for joy.

Parents should take the advice they give to their children: Stop, Look and Listen.

become more enjoyable. Why wait? These moments can never be regained.

Overcommitted parents too easily skim across their days without plucking the everyday opportunities for happiness that are theirs for the taking. But children hold no grudges for past omissions. They will accept their parents into their world of enjoyment for any amount of time.

Parents can breeze in to enjoy a quick game of cards, a walk to the store, a round of catch or an old-fashioned race. Or, they can stay longer for a swim, a bicycle ride, or an hour on the tennis court. Children are even willing to join traditional adult pastimes, such as cooking meals, cleaning out attics, or eating out in enjoyable restaurants. Creative nights can energize families who read ghost stories by candlelight, or play flashlight hide-and-seek indoors on a dark, winter night. When parents cannot think of possibilities, most children are pleased to help; just ask.

DOING NOTHING except watching children enjoy their own games can, at times, be the most fun. Mothers and fathers who quietly walk into their child's bedroom may be stepping into a world of adventure. Parents should take the advice they give to their children: Stop, Look and Listen. Enjoy watching the artists of happiness. If parents are patient, their children may soon direct them into their world of play.

Having fun should not be work. But for those who are out of the habit of having fun, a commitment must be made to practice. Parents need to disembark from the train to the future and dedicate 15, 30 or more minutes per day to enjoying family living. At first, parents may feel awkward but, like riding a bicycle, the skills of happy living quickly return. Soon parents no longer will need to remind themselves to have daily fun with the family. It will come naturally. After all, "happiness is not a goal one reaches, but a way of travel."

PITFALL 13
"I GUESS THIS MEANS I'LL HAVE TO GO CAMPING"

"I guess this means I'll have to go camping." Not at all. Each family must find its own ways to have fun. Possibilities vary. Some enjoy camping in the wilderness; others prefer to stay in hotels in major cities. Some delight in cooking together while others are fond of dining in favorite restaurants. Some play sports at home, and others relish watching professional sports. Some read aloud from Edgar Allen Poe or Dr. Seuss, while many share articles from *Scientific America*.

Each family develops a family character for having fun. Like fingerprints and snowflakes, no two families' methods will be the same. What is important is not how a family has fun together, but that they enjoy the journey together, that their travel is happy. Step down from the train to the future. If you wish to travel happily through life, board a train that makes daily stops. ALL ABOARD!

MYTH 14

DON'T LAY YOUR VALUES ON YOUR CHILDREN

Do you know who is teaching values to your children today? I hope the answer is that *you* are. In the '60s a new myth crept into parenting circles like Kudzu spreads over the Southern countryside: "Don't lay your values on your children."

The myth encouraged parents to allow their children to learn values through "self-discovery." But values don't suddenly emerge from within; they arise through interaction with people and ideas. If parents sidestep the opportunity to teach values to their children, then someone else or some other force will take over this responsibility.

If parents decline the challenge to teach their children, perhaps the major portion of their instruction will be taken over by their children's peers, or television, videos and movies, or more aggressive people. A child without a moral foundation floats aimlessly in an ocean filled with predators, as well as some friendlier species. Although gentle creatures may act as guides through perilous waters, hostile man-eaters also lurk below — always ready to destroy the weak. Make sure your values

> A child without a moral foundation floats aimlessly in an ocean filled with predators, as well as some friendlier species.

assure your children of a relatively safe voyage through life.

Balance helps parents teach their values to children. A respect for the child's right to explore and think independently can be balanced with the teaching of sound family values. Moral training loses equilibrium when either teaching or experience becomes overemphasized. The movement by some toward permissive moral training may have occurred as a backlash response to those parents who indoctrinate their children with the help of an authoritarian hand. Many models for teaching values fall short of the desired balance.

Value Pounders package a specific set of values that they hammer into their children's psyches. Pounders insist that their values represent absolute truth and that conflicting viewpoints typify evil thinking. These parents must stand guard over their children's friends, entertainment and teachers lest a foreign idea be slipped through the family's defenses. By restricting their children's freedom of thought and experience, parents disrupt the desired balance in moral training. Emphasis shifts toward inculcating their values.

The Bradley family sent their children to public schools, but insisted to the administration that their family values should be taught there. Mr. and Mrs. Bradley gave Tommy (age eight) the third-degree when he returned from school each day. Mrs. Bradley led the interrogation with questions such as, "What did your teacher say?" or "What did you read?" After collecting evidence that inappropriate values had been taught, the Bradleys regularly called the principal with a list of demands for changing teacher behaviors and school curriculums.

The Bradley family lost their balance. They lacked the confidence that their children would internalize the family's values. Therefore, the Bradleys, like military police, kept close watch on their children when they entered civilian territory. Heavy censorship implies that

Respect for the child's right to explore and think independently can be balanced with the teaching of sound values.

Many families play "I've got a secret" with their values.

other values are inferior and dangerous. The Bradleys' martial law prevented their children from developing a tolerance for beliefs which differ from their own.

Erring in the opposite direction, many families play "I've got a secret" with their values. By stressing their children's right to intellectual and experiential freedom, overly "objective" parents feel embarrassed or guilty when teaching their beliefs to their children. These Professorial Parents strive to be "fair" by teaching — with impartiality — each side of a moral argument. For example, instead of sharing their personal beliefs about the morality of premarital sex, they offer their children a lecture in sociology. "Some people believe premarital sex is O.K.; others don't. I am not going to tell you my beliefs; you will have to work out yours on your own." Professorial Parents lose balance. In their quest for objectivity, they offer few beacons or landmarks to direct their children. Wandering through the wilderness, their children may find that survival is a struggle and lose their direction. Often, they needlessly suffer along the way.

Mr. James Q. Lawrence hid his religious beliefs from his children and friends. "To push my children toward my beliefs is unfair," professed Mr. Lawrence. Instead, James Q. Lawrence discussed with his children the value found in each of the world's major religions. As a consequence, the Lawrence children believed that all religious teachings shared general truth but that none was specifically correct. Following his guideline for non-interference in religious training, Mr. Lawrence avoided going to church, unless the children wished to attend — which was never. He avoided prayer, unless the children wished to pray — which was never. The Lawrence children never guessed that their father nourished deep and specific beliefs.

As adolescents, the children were shocked to discover that their dad had maintained strong religious beliefs throughout their childhoods. Every night, their father had read the Bible — in private. Regularly, Mr. Lawrence had prayed to request that God watch over his family, but his children never knew about his devotion. Mr. Lawrence hid his major values and taught his secondary values. Nothing was wrong with the values he taught his children, except that they did not represent his prized beliefs. James Q. Lawrence buried the religious treasure in his life, concealing it from those who could have profited most from his faith.

A variation on the invisible values game occurs when Rushed Parents "never get around to sharing their values." Parents who stay "on the go" may intend to share their beliefs and values, but never take time to do so. Discussions pertaining to drug use and sexual issues are delayed. Too many important engagements and opportunities prohibit Rushed Parents from finding time to teach values to their children — or even to take them to institutions or organizations that will teach them.

Occasionally, single parents and stepparents become uncomfortable with the values presented to their children by other adults who share their custody. They often feel pulled between remaining quiet about the differences that exist among adults and wishing to be outspoken. Adults need to share and model their beliefs directly, without condemning the beliefs of others. Children will be wise enough eventually to judge for themselves which adults lead healthy lives. But to assault the values of other adults whom children love may lead the youth to come to the defense of those attacked and to follow guidelines they really don't prefer. Do your best — share and model. At that point, your positive influence ends.

Probably the best known error of adults is to teach by the ancient standard, "Do as I say, not as I do." Parents may bombard their children with eloquent messages about sex, drugs, religion, and human rights. However, children clearly see when their parents' behaviors violate these moral commercials. We all know families like the Smythes.

James Q. Lawrence buried the religious treasure in his life, concealing it from those who could have profited most from his faith.

During her late teenage years, Rebecca, the Smythes' adolescent daughter, became drug dependent. The parents could not understand the origin of her addiction. "We always taught her about the evils of alcohol abuse and drug addiction," Mrs. Smythe declared. "In fact, we talked about the problems drugs can cause until we were blue in the face." Mrs. Smythe doesn't understand Rebecca's dependency; the Smythes' friends do.

Whenever Mr. Smythe returned home from a trying day, he loudly announced: "I need a double shot of scotch. What a day!" From Mr. Smythe, his children learned that drugs ease stress. At their parties, the Smythes always insured that alcohol flowed freely. From the Smythes, their children learned that drugs enhance social occasions. Mr. Smythe enjoyed bragging about his fraternity escapades of the past — the times when the brothers drank too much and played mischief around the campus. From Mr. Smythe, the children learned that drunks enjoy exciting adventures.

The Smythes presented their children with a double message. Verbally, they expressed reservations about the use of drugs. Behaviorally, they modeled a form of drug dependency. Rebecca was more impressed by what she saw her parents do than by what she heard them say. Mr. and Mrs. Smythes' moral training exemplified the motto: "To seem rather than to be."

Many parents strive throughout life to develop sound values. Sincere in their search, they frequently respond to a child's questions in regard to sexual or drug-related issues with the honest response: "I don't know what is true." The difficulty with this paradigm for teaching values is that children don't understand the message, and a parent's lack of specific answers may be interpreted to mean that all behaviors are of equal merit. Despite the honesty of these struggling parents, their children may need to roll the dice before making moral decisions.

Empty Parents — those without moral codes —

become the most unfortunate class of moral educators. Usually, their lack of values results from a family tradition of shallow moral training. With no value system to guide them through life, their decisions usually are based on what may bring instant gratification.

Without parental mentors, children learn values "on the street." Usually street training on moral issues proves to be poor. For example, how many times must young adolescents become pregnant because they "didn't think it could happen during their first sexual encounter." Shallow parents, ethically speaking, generally raise children with superficial values. Fault may not always lie with the parents — who have nothing to teach — but with a society that fails to break negative educational cycles that include poor moral training.

Don't lay your values on your child? If you don't, someone else will indoctrinate them with theirs.

**OLD AND IMPROVED BELIEF 14
PARENTS NEED TO TEACH AND
MODEL FAMILY VALUES**

Parents who share and model a specific value create a family value. Despite quests for uniqueness, each child in the family generally adopts the family's values. Studies of adolescents suggest that the majority of them share their parents' most prized values, although they may differ over minor issues such as tastes and fads. Success in creating a family value usually depends on whether BOTH parents model shared values.

Divorced parents, as well as married adults, can agree on family values they want to teach, and then insure that each parent models those beliefs. When parents model differing values, the family value is lost. Then each child must decide which parent's example to imitate. The

Gleason family provides a familiar example of what may occur when parents model two different ideals.

Although the Gleasons both explained to their children the importance of reading, only Mrs. Gleason made a habit of reading. Mr. Gleason preferred to watch televised news. He then tuned in the nightly sports programs. Nevertheless, Mr. Gleason continued to TELL his son Matthew (age eight) that reading was an important part of living. Matthew's sister Martha (age ten) enjoyed reading, but Matthew resisted. He refused to read or to do homework. Instead, he chose to watch a seemingly endless string of cartoons. Mrs. Gleason became annoyed: "Why can't both of them read and study? My husband and I both value reading and academics."

Wrong! Reading failed to become a family value because one parent rarely read. If Mr. Gleason had truly valued reading, then he would have read. Mr. Gleason values watching television. His son shares this value, and his daughter shares the mother's enjoyment of reading.

Family values help children make important decisions concerning school, drugs, sex, and religion. After parents establish a family value, they need to seek the balance between their need to teach morals and their child's right to think and to experience life with reasonable freedom. If parents become too forceful, they may challenge adolescents to rebel. Have confidence that your family values will take hold. Then keep the lines of communication open while children face the challenge of learning to apply values to life situations.

Below are examples of how a few parents created family values to help their children handle problems related to school, drugs, sex, and religion. You may differ with the specific values these parents taught. But what is important is not the parents' stances, but their desire to contribute family values to their children in these crucial areas of living.

The Harpers loved learning. Mr. and Mrs. Harper

When parents model differing values, the family value is lost. Then each child must decide which parent's example to imitate.

ignited interesting conversations about new events and new thoughts. They always displayed their support of their children's education by providing opportunities for their children to discuss their interests. The children's reports elicited enthusiastic responses from their parents. From their infancy, books were read nightly to the Harper children by BOTH Mr. and Mrs. Harper. Reading became a way of life.

At seven o'clock every night, the Harpers spent at least a half-hour reading. Often their interests kept them involved long after the reading period ended. Soon their reading time seemed to be as important as meal times. The Harpers' three children excelled in school in different areas, but excellence was not the children's goal. They simply followed the family value that learning is important. Excellence became a by-product of family values.

Another crucial question in most young people's lives is how they will respond to the challenge of alcohol and drug use. Most young people will receive an "invitation" to join those who use drugs. Unlike the Smythe family in an earlier example, many parents model the behaviors they hope their children will display. Some don't drink at all. Others teach moderation and actively oppose any excessive use.

The Greens enjoyed alcoholic beverages and decided to teach their children the virtues of moderation. At supper Mr. and Mrs. Green often enjoyed a glass of wine. Their children would beg for a taste. The Greens downplayed the request and offered them a sip. The children hated the taste. The Greens minimized the attention given to these and other minor episodes involving the family's use of alcohol.

On occasion, the Greens invited guests, and alcoholic drinks were served. At other times, guests were offered only non-alcoholic drinks. Both parents displayed their belief that social occasions without drugs are enjoyable. Knowing that adolescents attempt to outstrip their

> **Excellence became a by-product of family values.**

parents' adventures, the Greens never discussed exploits involving the use of alcohol. On every possible occasion, Mr. and Mrs. Green stressed the fact that drinking and driving do not mix.

As adolescents, the Greens' children showed little interest in using alcoholic beverages. Their parents' moderate approach neither made of alcohol a forbidden fruit nor an available product. Although parents satisfied their children's curiosity for tasting alcohol, they insisted that their children wait until the legal age before consuming alcoholic products. As adults, the Greens' children — predictably — became moderate drinkers.

While the Greens' approach might not prove satisfactory for your family, it met their goal for teaching the responsible use of alcohol. The Greens didn't wait for others to teach their children about the use of drugs. They knew that this area of moral education is a crucial one. Drugs can kill.

Sexual tests may become the most difficult challenge in a young person's life. Our society bears a dismal record in preventing unwanted pregnancies. Debates rage over the morality of premarital intercourse, as well as the suitability of sex education taught in the public schools. No national resolution appears at hand, despite the fact that Valueless Parents rarely prepare their children to make informed sexual decisions.

No matter what course society takes concerning sex education, abortion, or the availability of contraceptives, parents can help their children by creating family values. Specific values — as always — will vary from family to family, but generally adolescents will benefit from the family's united stance.

The Ashcrafts and Browns supported two different viewpoints in preparing their children to respond to sexual questions. The Ashcrafts believed that premarital sex should be discouraged but not condemned. They discussed with their children the dangers associated with

No matter what course society takes concerning sex education, abortion, or the availability of contraceptives, parents can help their children by creating family values.

premarital sexual intercourse. The Ashcrafts urged their children not to experiment with intercourse until after marriage. Nevertheless, they requested that their children come to them for contraceptives should the temptation become irresistible.

The Ashcrafts' close, honest relationship with their children allowed one of their children to approach them rather than peers during a time of crisis. At age 17 their son (deeply in love) asked Mr. Ashcraft for help. After a heart-to-heart discussion, Mr. Ashcraft helped his son buy contraceptives and instructed him on their proper use. Although the Ashcrafts were not pleased with their son's decision, they were happy that an unwanted pregnancy would not alter his life.

On the other hand, the Browns opposed premarital sexual intercourse for any reason. They taught their children this value and the logic that supported their stance. The Browns kept the door open for their children to come to them in the future. "You may have difficult challenges in the coming years. Please come to us. We care and we will help you" became the Browns' message.

During his late teen years one of the Browns' children came to his mother to discuss his strong sexual feelings. Without condemning his urges, his mother listened and discussed various possibilities. With the help of his mother's understanding and suggestions, the youth decided against engaging in sexual intercourse.

Both the Ashcrafts' and Browns' children avoided undesired pregnancies. True, many young people will not. But those whose parents are involved enjoy a greater likelihood of steering clear of errors. Parents with strong points of view need to express those views, then leave the door open for children to return for more conversations.

Erik Erikson's (the leading stage theorist of our era) contributions to developmental psychology include a conviction that parents must believe in something in order to pass on to their children a trust that life offers meaning

Don't be reluctant to share your most treasured beliefs. Or others — outside of your family — may pass their beliefs to your children.

and purpose. Parental beliefs greatly vary. For some, faith is found in formal religion, while for others it is found in their belief in mankind — for example, that people can and will solve the problems in their world with or without God's help. Beliefs that parents hold about life will spawn hope in their children. Don't be reluctant to share your most treasured beliefs. Or others — outside of your family — may pass their beliefs to your children.

NEW PITFALL 14 TEACHING TOO MUCH TOO SOON

"Wow! That's right. I need to share my values. My values are unique. I won't allow others to take over my child's moral education. Children! Come in here this minute. We have some serious issues to discuss."

Wait a moment! Timing is the key. Teach values as life offers the opportunities when critical moments for teaching arise. You need to look for them and be ready to share your beliefs. As for modeling your values, each day offers that opportunity.

The story circulates about the mother who was anxious to teach her children about sexuality. She collected books and pictures that vividly displayed all anyone might need to know about sex. Impatiently, she waited to do her duty. One day her second-grade son came home from school and asked, "Mom, where did I come from?" Finally, the time for sex education had arrived. The mother hustled her child into a private room and began her graphic lesson.

Wide-eyed and interested, the child looked up after the conclusion and said: "That was great. Can we do it again?" Confidently, the mother replied, "Certainly, always feel you can come to me with your questions."

"O.K.," responded her son, "I do have one more question." The mother beamed. Then the child began: "Where did I come from? My best friend, Jake, comes from Chicago."

Don't be overly anxious. Wait for the proper moment, then never teach more than your child can understand and emotionally handle.

Don't be overly anxious. Wait for the proper moment, then never teach more than your child can understand and emotionally handle.

MYTH 15

BOYS WILL BE BOYS

"Boys will be boys" — as we all know — is the most frequently offered apology from parents who have lost control of their sons' behaviors. This myth and the attendant folklore suggest that males are driven by an untrainable, if not uncontrollable, nature. Acceptance of this myth relieves parents of the responsibility for broadening their sons' behaviors, values, and inclinations. As a result, a male's possibilities shrink to fit the outmoded Macho-Success role. What follows in life will be future apologies, such as, "Isn't it just like a man?" "Your dad doesn't know how to tell you this, but . . ." "He's all thumbs in the kitchen," and, "That's a man's world out there."

The need for the kind of male liberation that will allow boys to develop and expand their capabilities provides this chapter's emphasis. Nothing will prove more important to families than for males to receive the training needed before they can fulfill a wide variety of roles that support the family. As women move with more flexibility toward their future roles, they must be met by adaptable men who are able to keep in step with the needs of a changing family. If the training of young males lags behind that of females, then future husbands and fathers will dance awkwardly to the tunes of modern families.

For decades, the "boys will be boys" mentality forced males into a Macho-Success role that offered little or no flexibility. Males were trained to burst forth from school with a momentum that would propel them to the top of their chosen professions. Collecting a wife and child along the way helped, as long as these didn't draw too much time away from the pursuit of success.

Because of their upbringing and professional ambitions in the past, males rarely developed the ability to care for children. Most traditional males, for example, seem to display child-raising skills and stamina that endure for less than four or five hours while on solo "flights" with their children. After this period, traditional fathers may feel overwhelmed with their caretaking responsibilities. In addition, the "boys will be boys" trap prevented most traditional males from providing the emotional support that many children and teens need. In general, men were unprepared to meet the changing needs of the family that were produced by social and economic forces of the late twentieth century.

Times changed; women demanded equal opportunities to succeed professionally as well as more equality in the distribution of work at home. Little girls now are trained to believe that they can be corporate presidents as well as mothers. The women's movement assaulted the Macho-Success fortress. The walls cracked but did not fall. Women changed; men budged.

Families changed also. Divorce rates soared and left many adults struggling in their new roles as single parents or stepparents. The needs of families changed so swiftly that society failed to keep pace. As a symbol of society's slowness, latchkey children — school children who remain unsupervised between the end of the school day and their parent's arrival home from work — have

> **Because of their upbringing and professional ambitions in the past, males rarely developed the ability to care for children.**

become a phenomenon that still pricks our nation's conscience. These children need help, but no one in society seems willing to take responsibility. As a result, children remain alone behind locked doors or roam aimlessly through city streets.

The ideal is that children — male and female — must be trained to fulfill *a wide variety of roles* to meet the changing needs of families. Flexibility will be the key to a family's survival and future success. Males and females alike should be prepared to become the major breadwinner, the dominant caretaker, or a combination of the two. For males to accomplish this broadening of preparation, they must abandon the Macho-Success tradition.

True, many males raised by past myths will continue to find marriages and families that cater to those myths. Well-prepared for this dance, they will encounter no conflicts or awkwardness as long as the dance floor is not rocked by unexpected change. Families fueled by the Macho-Success traditions may live contented and meaningful lives in the new age. But for the vast majority of American families, social and economic forces already have changed their lives. In fact, some estimate that less than five to seven percent of families follow the traditional pattern of women staying at home while their husbands establish careers. Working mothers and full-time daycare are the realities of modern life.

Trying to adjust to unforeseen changes, many males have attempted to make personal transformations that could benefit their families. But lack of the early training that is required to establish broad values and skills interfered with their success. For example, many men raised by the "boys will be boys" mythology never escape a feeling that their increased child-raising responsibilities are a hindrance to their lives rather than an opportunity to have stronger family relationships. Similarly, many men are unable to consider the completion of chores to be a

True, many males raised by past myths will continue to find marriages and families that cater to those myths.

shared responsibility among family members, rather than a favor a husband does for his spouse.

How did males become so addicted to the Macho-Success role? Many forces contributed to the Narrowing Process. In many cases, women played a significant part because of their own male-female stereotypes. In the past, many women were attracted to the "tall Pale Rider" who bore his troubles in silence while solving the problems of cowardly townfolks. Years later those attracted to the mysterious, quiet waters became dissatisfied. Wives asked, "Why can't my husband communicate better? Why can't he share his problems with me?" Children complained: "Dad could never be close to me or feel comfortable touching me. He rarely said, 'I love you.' "

Now the times call for a loving, caring male who is skilled in the arts of verbal and non-verbal communications. Families need fathers who are close by and make a commitment to the family. Males have ridden into the sunset — away from their families — for too long. The strong differentiation between masculine and feminine traits and roles trapped males for decades. Males conformed to the expectations that they be emotionally incompetent, just as many women pretended to need three guesses to discover how to hold a screwdriver and turn a screw in the proper direction. The old stereotypes find little support today. Genetic studies, for example, have presented no evidence that women have a predisposition to dive elbow deep into toilets, nor that men's tongues swell in their heads when tender emotions arise. Competencies in the home and the work place appear to be learned, human competencies. Positive personality traits are neither masculine nor feminine.

Modern parents avoid much of the traditional stereotyping that afflicted young girls. Now, equal attention needs to be focused on the Narrowing Process for males. For example, parents may encourage their daughters to play sports but still deny their sons the opportunity to

Parents begin the paralysis process; teachers continue it.

nurture dolls. Adults avoid giving domestic toys, such as tea sets and stoves, to boys but continue to give them toys of war, such as guns and toy soldiers. While dependency is tolerated in girls, little boys are allowed, if not encouraged, to be aggressive. Parents, often unwittingly, continue the "boys will be boys" tradition as the first step in the Narrowing Process.

Parents begin the paralysis process; teachers continue it. Studies report that teachers expect and push males to succeed; girls receive less encouragement. Expecting more progress from males, teachers demand higher standards in their work. Although in the early grades girls excel in their performances on tests, by graduation time males have overtaken them because they live up to the expectations and demands of their teachers. Those expectations clearly suggest that a man's place is in the business world. The cementing of males into the stereo-typical role is seen even in their play. Males of elemen-tary-school age play competitive games that emphasize dominance and victory. On the other hand, girls play games, according to Carol Gilligan of Harvard, that stress human relationships, games that involve inclusion and exclusion from an inner circle of friends. The division seems apparent: girls will be relationship oriented and males will be competitive and ambitious.

Peer groups support the Narrowing Process. If a young boy becomes too sensitive for other males and expresses his emotions freely, his peer group may call him a sissy or a nerd — a warning to conform to the "boys will be boys" standard. Women who are assertive and athletic may be called "tomboys," or worse, and may be excluded from more "feminine groups." If boys and girls continue to stray too far beyond the barrier of their peers' toleration of differences, titles such as "gay," "lesbos" or "fags" are used to punish them. These titles show an insensitivity not only to peers, but also to those in society who differ from the majority.

The Narrowing Process shoves males and females toward stereotyped occupations with little regard for the individual's goals and values. For example, in a graduate admissions meeting I attended, the committee considered an application from a male who listed his professional ambition to be that of an "assistant principal." Many of the faculty present openly questioned what might be wrong with a young man whose life long ambition was to be an assistant principal rather than a principal. A woman who shared the same goal might not have evoked similar questions. Why? Because the "boys will be boys" tradition lives. Committee members assume that a woman might have career ambitions that would allow her to spend more time at home with her family. But males who prefer to commit their time and energy to their families appear to be peculiar.

Males in nontraditional families face special challenges. Boys in single parent homes often lack a male model. They must guess what it is to be a man. Often, young boys overcompensate and become too aggressive. In many cases their mothers seem reluctant to set and enforce limits. As a result, both the mothers and sons are likely to become victims of the myth that "boys will be boys."

The "boys will be boys" myth played a central role in limiting males to behaviors and feelings representative of the Macho- Success system. But now everyone has the right to develop values, attributes and skills that will allow them maximum flexibility in meeting life's unexpected challenges.

**No longer will a
person's worth
be a measure
of individual
achievement
alone.**

**NEW AND IMPROVED BELIEF 15
BOYS CAN BE MORE**

To promote and enjoy family life in the future, males must escape from, and eliminate, the Narrowing Process. Their release from the Macho-Success role requires a major shift in values. No longer will a person's worth be a measure of individual achievement alone. Instead, worth will be placed on each person's ability to cooperate in a way that will allow each family member to succeed. Young people need parents who are dedicated to providing the structure, constancy and, most of all, the time and love that the young require in order to flourish.

Women's professional progress and the resultant changes in the home have sparked a variety of reactions. Males who are most entrenched in male mythology insist that women revert to their old ways and abandon progress. Others poke fun at broadly trained males for not sliding through the narrow pass to male "supremacy." Unable to accept cooperative living and the flexibility required to assume a variety of roles, many cling to a restricted way of living.

Many males have followed the lead of females and have begun the struggle to learn new roles never modeled by their parents. Some males not only lacked early training but also failed to take advantage of educational possibilities to learn about family life. Until recently, seats in child development and parenting classes were filled predominantly with women. Even when struggling as parents, traditional males sidestepped parenting courses with the attitude that "no one is going to tell me how to parent my kids, no matter how miserable my family may become." Modern males now attend classes as part of their commitment to expand their capabilities.

Contemporary males understand the value of becoming more sensitive, caring and communicative. In the past, fathers were less involved in child care; consequently, their more authoritarian methods appeared to be successful. Children often conformed to their fathers' wills knowing that their dads would soon leave home to meet the demands of their careers or recreational interests. Increased time spent with children now requires that males abandon authoritarian and more aggressive techniques and employ techniques of discipline and communication that build high self-esteem and self-confidence in a child. It is no longer enough to walk into the home after work, dispense discipline, then walk away; fathers must nurture their children.

This transition toward a commitment to meet the needs of children arrives, unfortunately, at a time when the parenting profession earns little positive regard. In recent years, adults abandoned the role of parenting in the same way that the middle class formerly fled from the city. Most adults seek recognition outside of the home. But many authors believe that as males seek to balance the opportunities for all family members to succeed, their resulting increased commitment to the home will raise the value of parenting. Also, many contemporary fathers who stumble in their attempt as adults to escape from the Macho-Success myth may be more successful in training their sons to be free of the "boys will be boys" web.

This generation of parents can offer their sons new flexibility and freedom. A first step will require that sons display socially appropriate behaviors — the civilized behavior most parents already require of their daughters. Rules that require children to respect the rights of others create a stable foundation on which responsibility and love can grow. Expecting acceptable behavior counters the old "boys will be boys" mythology that implies that males naturally misbehave. Males no longer can become intoxicated with their "right" to follow their own desires and ambitions without serious regard for the needs of

In the past, fathers were less involved in child care; consequently, their more authoritarian methods appeared to be successful.

others. There should no longer be two standards for behavior based on sex.

Young males, as well as females, need to become assertive, not passive or aggressive. In the past, females were expected to be passive and males were expected to be aggressive. As a result, aggressive males often lacked an appreciation for the rights and feelings of others, while passive females displayed little regard for themselves. Assertive children will no longer err in either extreme. Children must be taught to make decisions that respect their own rights and the rights of others. Those who are raised within a climate of cooperation and mutual respect are more likely, as adults, to make decisions that will benefit everyone.

Males must continue to develop their techniques for communicating positive feelings. In other cultures, males hug children, friends and colleagues without self-consciousness. Their embraces clearly convey love and concern. But in our mainline society, males appear less comfortable expressing tenderness or vulnerability, either verbally or physically. This narrowness resulted from the unfortunate rule that robbed men of the right to express sensitive and vulnerable feelings. The "boys will be boys" mythology left males emotionally handicapped and women with the responsibility of conveying love for both parents. Communication of feelings, both verbally and non-verbally, is a human expression, not a feminine one.

Play offers many males an opportunity to practice caring for others. Dolls, teddy bears, and pets provide opportunities to practice nurturing skills. Fathers need to support the delicate play of their children. A father's acceptance of his son's sensitivities acknowledges that they are strengths, not weaknesses. When fathers model these characteristics, as well as affirm them, then young males increase their likelihood of becoming sensitive fathers. Sensitive males contribute to the smooth running of their homes.

Aggressive males often lacked an appreciation for the rights and feelings of others, while passive females displayed little regard for themselves.

Caring for every aspect of a home can be learned early in life. It is a myth that males and females should perform an equal amount of work around the house. Cooperative couples will divide the work according to the family's present need. What is important is that young children know how to perform as many jobs and tasks around the house as possible. Then, as adults they will be better able to serve the family. In the past, the Narrowing Process prevented most males from becoming competent in the kitchen or laundry room. Some men not only could not cook, but never learned how to turn on the washing machine. Young males did learn to cut the grass and take out the trash. Sometimes they forgot to complete these simple chores; but after all, "boys will be boys." All children should be expected to learn to be competent in every area of home and yard care. Distribution of tasks and training periods can be scheduled in family meetings, as we shall see later.

Parents may teach children most by how they choose to use their time. The use of time, rather than money, is the measure of a contemporary adult's commitment. When fathers spend time nourishing their marriage and their children, then children know that relationships are important. Fathers who work overtime, then hide behind the shield of "quality time" do not fool their children, although they may deceive themselves.

Schools need to join in the Broadening Process by eliminating the traditional methods that helped to confine men to the Macho-Success role. Sensitivity can be encouraged through the use of affective educational techniques. Professions such as nursing and law should be viewed as possible careers for both sexes. In order to bring about change, schools need to provide in-service workshops to help teachers avoid blatant and subtle stereotyping in the classroom. University education departments must train teachers to encourage students toward the same high goals, regardless of sex. Schools

> **Caring for every aspect of a home can be learned early in life.**

need to emphasize the legitimacy, if not the necessity, of males becoming dedicated to family living.

Schools could be mandated, given proper financing, to meet stressful family and societal needs. Supervision and structure could be provided for latchkey children. Dual-career parents need more evening conference possibilities with teachers. The common needs of those who experience similar circumstances — such as children from single parent homes and stepfamilies — could be discussed in small groups. Family life classes could be offered to all students, not just teenaged parents. Schools can play a crucial role in needed social change.

Families have changed; men need to respond with a leap, not a budge. By developing the flexibility to be the major caretaker, or the major breadwinner, or a combination, men will serve their family's needs with more efficiency. By joining forces with women, men can insist that laws, schools and agencies move to meet the changing needs of families. "Boys will be boys" — only in a world gone by.

**NEW PITFALL 15
YOU CANNOT HAVE IT ALL**

For years, women struggled with the question: "Can I have everything at once: children, a good marriage, a prosperous career and time for personal growth?" Many in the Second Wave of Women's liberation say: "No. There is not enough time." When men in the past asked the same question of themselves: "Can I have it all?" their answer was, "Yes." Why? Because in the past women accepted the major responsibility for their children and the home.

In the future, men may not be free to fulfill all of their dreams at once. Any father who spends significant amounts of time with his family pays a price, usually in his profession. For every hour that a father devotes to his children, spends with his wife, or fulfills domestic roles, another male will be working to promote a career. Men who try to have it all will become frustrated — until society changes its values, training programs and career opportunities.

When adults demand that the restrictive elements of society accommodate the new needs of families, then the challenges of raising a family will ease. Men may not be happier after they change their values, but they will receive the enjoyment of participating in their family's growth in exchange for any alterations they make.

We live in a society where no one — not women, not men and not children — can "have it all" any more. But through joint commitment, families can work together so everyone can reach reasonable personal goals.

MYTH 16

CHILDREN ARE MORE LIKE ADULTS IN THEIR THINKING THAN IN THEIR FEELINGS

Faddish gurus push parents to transform their child into a Mozart, an Emily Dickinson, an Albert Einstein, an Aristotle. The cost of early enrollments in kiddy colleges for infants and four-year-olds or academic pressure for first and second-graders may be — at the least — the joys of childhood. Those who press to accelerate children's learning do so in vain and at the expense of the child.

Once basic educational needs for age-appropriate challenges are met, children's intellectual abilities unfold at their own rate. Thinking cannot be hurried. Any parent who has listened to a four-year-old explain the existence of God, or an eight-year-old discuss politics understands this age-related unfolding. Children do not develop complex skills for thought until their teen-aged years. Before that time, adults often overestimate their children's thinking.

Children, however, do experience feelings similar to their parents'. Their feelings are hurt when they are talked to rudely, they grow jealous over unequal treatment, they become angry when they don't receive what they want, they become discouraged when they are on the losing end of a comparison, and they love their parents intensely enough to forgive them for almost any offense. Children experience most emotions felt by adults. These emotions, unlike thinking skills, do not unfold slowly. True, it requires many years of experience for children to learn to use their emotions positively and to manage complex emotions such as despair or grief. Nevertheless, many adults overlook the ability of their children to feel emotions and, therefore, treat them with a lack of respect.

Below is a typical example of the frustration an adult encounters when trying to impart complex information to children of different ages. Each child's response is predictable and age-appropriate.

After Mrs. Gibson decided to end her marriage, she wanted to share the facts leading to her divorce with her children. She called them together — Sally (eight months), Paul (four years), James (eight years), and Meredith (fourteen years) and delivered a carefully prepared speech.

"Children, I want you to hear something directly from me because I love you very much. Your father and I have found it difficult to live happily together for some time. We finally decided that it would be best for all of us if we got a divorce. I want you to understand why we are divorcing.

"Your dad and I never could agree about finances. He always felt we needed more money. So he began working overtime and soon he was at work more than he was at home. He began spending a lot of time with his secretary — you know Sue — and they fell in love. Of course, I couldn't live with him under those conditions so we agreed to a divorce. I do want you to know that both your father and I love you very much. Our divorce has nothing to do with you. He will be happy to tell you about his feelings when you see him. Now, I want to make sure you

> **Many adults overlook the ability of their children to feel emotions and, therefore, treat them with a lack of respect.**

have a chance to ask questions. What would you like to know?"

Sally (eight months) responded by crawling over to her toys and playing. She had listened to her mother because her mom sounded so serious. However, Mrs. Gibson correctly anticipated that Sally would not understand. Paul (four years) asked, "So will Sue be coming to live with us?" James (eight years) interrupted, "Don't be so stupid, Paul. Of course not. I just want to say that I think Dad is a total jerk, and I don't plan to talk to him or Sue ever again." These were not the reactions Mrs. Gibson anticipated; she began to feel the wheels coming off her careful plan. After a moment, Meredith quietly asked: "Mom, have you and Dad considered going to a marriage counselor? Maybe there is some way to pull things back together again. Maybe there are problems other than those with Sue and money." Floored by Meredith's observations and advice, Mrs. Gibson began to sob.

Mrs. Gibson had delivered a well-planned speech. With an audience of adults, her strategy might have been successful; however, her children did not react as adults. Why? Because she overestimated Paul's and James' ability to understand her situation and she underestimated Meredith's abilities. Unless Mrs. Gibson now discusses the situation individually with each child and in terms they might understand, then her children's thoughts and emotions may flounder. In the end, Mrs. Gibson's heart-to-heart talk may create the difficulties she hoped to prevent.

Children's thoughts differ from adults' in predictable ways. Knowing the differences adds enjoyment to adults' lives and diminishes frustration for both adults and children. For example, a four-year-old's vivid imagination inspires play in the daytime but ignites fears and nightmares in the evening. Adults can cause problems by ignoring a child's imagination. I recall, for example, the story of a kindly Christian babysitter who told her wards not to be frightened at night because the Holy Ghost would be in the room with them. Of course, the children stayed awake most of the night, terrified that an invisible ghost was roaming through their bedroom. Most adults can only begin to understand complex religious ideas, and for all adults these ideas usually remain challenging, if not confusing.

The lying of an eight-year-old provides another example of the age-related challenges awaiting adults. If eight-year-olds lie and then repeat the lie several times, they soon believe it to be the truth. Almost all adults — whether parents, teachers or administrators — have "caught a child in a lie" only to have the beleaguered youngster fight them with righteous indignation. "I did not steal her allowance. I found this money in my lunch box," claims the child. After repeated testimonies to that effect, the petty thief soon believes his own story despite eyewitness accounts to the contrary.

Like adults, children feel love, hurt, hate, humiliation, happiness, anger, embarrassment, ecstasy and even depression. Being unaware of children's sensitivities, adults may unknowingly treat them with insensitivity. Adults should ask themselves, "Do I treat my child with the same respect that I treat my best friends?"

Often the tone of voice shows an adult's lack of respect. For example, a father may yell at his children for leaving their dirty dishes in the den, but moments later he may issue a kind request to his wife that she remove her dishes from the same room. Why does his wife receive special treatment? Because her husband respects her feelings, and also because he knows that she will not tolerate any insensitivity. His children are not able to demand the same respect, although their father's tone may hurt them just as badly.

Examples of disrespect abound. Nagging, using comparisons and public criticism, embarrassing children in

> **Like adults, children feel love, hurt, hate, humiliation, happiness, anger, embarrassment, ecstasy and even depression.**

Nagging, using comparisons and public criticism, embarrassing children in front of their peers — all are offenses that few adults would tolerate.

front of their peers —all are offenses that few adults would tolerate. In each case, children may feel hurt, humiliated, or discouraged. In response, they may retaliate with anger or revenge, as Myth #11 explains.

Fortunately, society is progressing rapidly in its acceptance of the importance of children's feelings. In most instances, adults try to be sensitive and considerate, even though their patience often runs thin. Society has been slower in recognizing the limitations of a child's thought. New Belief #16 will highlight a few of the significant characteristics of children's thought at different ages. Keeping a child's limitations in mind should liberate adults from the insensitive myth that children are more like adults in their thinking than in their feelings.

NEW AND IMPROVED BELIEF 16 "CHILDREN ARE MORE LIKE US IN THEIR FEELINGS THAN IN THEIR THINKING"

Why did Mrs. Gibson's children react so differently? Because children journey through three distinct worlds of thought that are unlike the world of most adult thinking. Jean Piaget, the famous Swiss psychologist, opened up these worlds for us in ways that increase our understanding of both the pleasures and limitations of each period. The reactions of Mrs. Gibson's children were predictable.

As a parent and psychologist, Jean Piaget observed that at similar ages children made similar mistakes in solving problems. As time passed, these particular mistakes were no longer made; children had reached a higher stage or period. Piaget's work led to the discovery that children journey through predictable, orderly periods of thought that cannot be accelerated. That is why most four-year-olds share similar characteristics in thinking that differ radically from the cognitive skills of an eight-year-old or a one-year-old.

Advances in age never insure that a higher stage will be reached. Genetic potential or brain damage limits some children's advancement. Severely deprived environments that provide inadequate stimulation can limit others. In addition, some children progress more quickly than their peers. As a result, a teacher may have a class of like-aged children who represent different worlds of thought. Each of Piaget's periods emphasizes that children are not like adults in their thinking.

PERIOD 1: Sensorimotor Period
(Birth to About 18 Months)

Parents usually understand that at this age a child's ability to think is limited. Almost no adult would expect a one-year-old to exhibit an interest in religion, morality or politics. In the example that began this chapter, Mrs. Gibson, of course, displayed no surprise when she found that her eight-month-old was oblivious to important life events.

Parents may not overestimate their child's capability for thought during the first 18 months, but adults may not fully appreciate it. Children learn by doing. Putting toys, sand and objects in their mouths allows them to discover the world around them. The mouth is a center for learning about taste and texture. Major discoveries occur during these months. For example, the complicated concept of permanence is learned. Children change from the belief that "out of sight is out of existence," to a belief in permanence that allows them to ransack their mother's pocketbook in search of hidden gum. Parents tuned to the child's struggle to understand permanence will enjoy playing peek-a-boo or jack-in-the-box with their child. Watch as a parent hides; the face of the child reflects a

Parents may not overestimate their child's capability for thought during the first 18 months, but adults may not fully appreciate it.

sincere fear that the adult is gone. With the parent's return, joy fills the face of the astonished child.

Experimentation also allows infants to learn about other scientific concepts, such as gravity. By dropping objects repeatedly to the floor — much to the dismay of some parents — children learn about a complex law of nature. In 18 months, children move from being an instinctive animal with few cognitive skills, to a toddler who can see a temper tantrum, remember it, then duplicate it in a similar situation two weeks later. At about 18 months, when children can use symbols such as words or visual pictures, they move into a new period of thought.

PERIOD 2: The Preoperational Period (Ages 18 Months to 7 Years)

This period of thought generates the memories parents recall for a lifetime: bears that walk, adventures that inspire, dolls that talk, and many memorable words and phrases. But the thinking of a child can confuse adults; children seem to understand more than they actually do. An explosion in language occurs between the ages of two and five that allows children to produce complicated words and terms. However, this dramatic increase in the vocabulary and imagination does not usher in sophisticated, adult thinking. Children often sound more sophisticated than they are.

For example, a four-year-old's thought exhibits several characteristics that complicated Mrs. Gibson's chore of explaining her divorce. Self-centeredness abounds in children at this stage; they overestimate their influence and significance. For example, while in this period children commonly believe that the sun exists solely for their purposes: to warm them and to give them light. This sense of self-importance may also lead them to believe that they are responsible for divorces, tragedies, and other

This sense of self-importance may also lead them to believe they are responsible for major life occurrences.

major life occurrences. Mrs. Gibson needed to anticipate such a reaction from Paul and move quickly to relieve his sense of responsibility.

Preoperational children's heavy imaginations lend belief to fairy tales and life to super heroes. To them a dream may come true if a child — like Cinderella — wishes hard enough. This attribute charms adults; it also can create problems. For example, a child may harbor a belief that someday divorced parents will reunite and the family will drift off together into a Walt Disney sunset. Such dreams can persist for years, despite parental attempts to combat them. Mrs. Gibson must beware.

Primitive logic accompanies the thought of this period. For example, children assume that any two things that occur close in time must have a strong cause-and-effect relationship. When a child is asked, "Why does that big boat float?" the response may be, "Because it's heavy." Then, looking at a sunken boat a child may reply to the same question: "It sank because it's heavy." Again Mrs. Gibson must be careful. Her four-year-old may believe that an event that occurred directly before dad left home actually caused his departure. So often I hear young children mistakenly confess, "Dad left home because I yelled (cried, hit, etc.) at him."

Preoperational children operate in their egocentric world that is filled with magic and excitement. It is a world with few rules and limited logic. Parents, like Mrs. Gibson, will remember highlights from this stage for a lifetime. But they must be aware that the beauty of the stage often is beset by thorny challenges.

PERIOD 3: Concrete Operations (Age 7-11 and Many Adults)

Can these be the same children who charmed their way through the preoperational period? The imagination

People seem to be either good or bad, smart or dumb, friends or enemies, or whatever dichotomy seems appropriate.

and magic of those early years vanishes: teddy bears are replaced by video games. Concrete operators — whether children or adults — tend to view their world in absolutes, in black and white. Complexity (or the gray areas that clutter life) lies beyond a child's understanding. Instead, to them people seem to be either good or bad, smart or dumb, friends or enemies, or whatever dichotomy seems appropriate. Nothing is subtle about the thinking during this period.

Mrs. Gibson faces a different set of challenges in working with her eight-year-old, James. Care must be taken to prevent one of the parents from becoming the villain, while the other appears to be blameless. A concrete operator's need for simplicity may lead James to the view that his dad's absence from home was the sole cause for the divorce: "Therefore, the divorce must be Dad's fault; therefore, Dad must not love us; therefore, Dad must be bad." Of course divorces follow complex interactions that even the couple involved rarely understands. Concrete operators do not handle complexity well; they find simple causes for complex problems.

Another challenging characteristic of this period — called cognitive conceit — leads children to act as if they are superior to their parents. Usually this conceit follows an error that parents or other adults make in the presence of an intolerant child. For example, when a teacher misspells a word, students may laugh and be convinced that the teacher is unintelligent. In Mrs. Gibson's case, her children's cognitive conceit may surface when she gives advice to them about relationships. A typical response from James might be highly sarcastic, such as, "And I guess you have done so well with relationships, that you can tell me what to do."

After a person in the concrete operational world reaches a conclusion, all evidence will be manipulated to support that notion. Evidence to the contrary will be ignored or distorted. If James, for example, believes that his father is the villain in the divorce, then everything Mr. Gibson does may be viewed in a negative light. Soon reports will be filed about Mr. Gibson's nasty apartment, his undesirable girlfriend, or his inflammatory rhetoric. Good reports will not be forthcoming.

Concrete operational thought allows children to learn skills based on rules and simple logic. These skills and their increased knowledge will serve them well throughout their lives. But at this point complex thought is not understood or, for that matter, found to be interesting. Children at this age grow bored during speeches, sermons, plays or movies that are not action-packed.

Parents must not overestimate their children's insightfulness. When talking to a child in this concrete operational period, adults must be explicit. Spell out the gray areas as clearly as possible, if a child needs to understand them. Do not allow children to adopt mistaken notions or they will collect sufficient evidence to support them.

> Children at this age grow bored during speeches, sermons, plays or movies that are not action-packed.

PERIOD 4: The Period of Formal Operations (60% of Adults, Begins as Early as Age 12)

From the simple, black-and-white thinking of concrete operations, those in formal operations move to a world where all thoughts seem possible. Now the gray areas of life can be understood. Adolescents enjoy thinking and, at times, may appear to create more problems with their thinking than they solve. Indeed adolescents might consider two thousand explanations for why their favorite boy friend or girl friend "looked funny at me" during lunch. Although their social skills and life experiences may be too limited to allow them to discover the truth, they do at least consider most of the possibilities.

Now students understand symbolism. Teachers can lecture without a fear of boring students who experience difficulty in understanding complex ideas. In discussions, adolescents in this period may offer unique viewpoints — some, perhaps, that adults have never considered. For example, following Mrs. Gibson's explanation of her divorce, Meredith challenged her mother by suggesting counseling and implying that the fault might not all be Dad's. Religious, political, and moral values are scrutinized by adolescents, and many different views, often unfriendly to family teachings, may be investigated.

Teenagers' ability to handle their emotions develops more slowly than their thinking. For example, teens may understand the facts associated with sexual intercourse, but be unable to handle the emotional overload that often accompanies sexual involvement. Lagging emotional development is one of the reasons that sexual intercourse among consenting teens generally works out poorly. Mrs. Gibson must be careful not to overestimate Meredith's ability to cope with the divorce. Although understandable to the teenager, such events may place Meredith on an emotional roller coaster.

The new belief suggests that children are more like parents in their feelings than in their thinking. A child's mental reaction to information in every area of life varies dramatically according to the child's age and its accompanying period of thought. Nevertheless, their emotions vary less; they express the same feelings their parents do, although they may not understand or handle their emotions as well. For the sake of their children, parents need to adopt the new and improved belief that "children are more like adults in their feelings than in their thinking."

NEW PITFALL 16
TO SHELTER CHILDREN FROM PAINFUL EMOTIONS, HIDE COMPLICATED HUMAN EVENTS

Children should not be sheltered from life events. Respect for a child's feelings does not imply that he should be sheltered from stressful feelings. Life parades events before us that arouse both pleasant and unpleasant emotions. To shelter children delays the opportunity for them to learn to cope with difficult feelings, often until a time when a supportive adult is not present to help.

Parents need to present challenging information in a manner that acknowledges the limitations in children's thinking and shows a sensitivity to their feelings. Sensitive parents will provide the love, support and encouragement required by a child to handle difficult life situations.

Lack of respect for a child's ability to handle life often increases family problems. For example, one mother told me that she stayed in her marriage for two years longer than she wanted to because she didn't believe her children could handle the divorce. But the two years proved more difficult than a divorce might have, and constant fighting and frequent depressions created a joyless home. Children are resilient. They adjust to life changes, as long as their parents can.

Do not feel sorry for children. Be empathetic and have the respect for them that displays a confidence that they will adapt to difficult situations. After explaining the facts, in an age-appropriate way, attend to their emotional needs in a supportive way. In time they may grow to understand the complexity of life, but for now their feelings already reflect complexity.

MYTH 17

ALWAYS STRIVE TO BE THE BEST

Somehow the myth — "always strive to be THE BEST" — weaseled into the American consciousness to dwell alongside legitimate beliefs that encourage support for underdogs, love of family, and the duty to follow one's conscience. Most ideals, including those that urge people to develop their talents or to strive for success, prove beneficial to those who hold them. However, the "strive to be THE BEST" myth lures competitors into an endless series of unproductive battles in their attempts to display superiority over friends and foes.

This myth, however, is good for the economy. Companies invest thousands of dollars promoting the idea that one electric can-opener opens cans better, faster, and more easily than any competitor's! A victory in the race to be THE BEST can-opener earns millions of dollars for the winning company. Likewise, polls and surveys that rate television shows, movies or products financially make or break high-quality programs and products. Winners in THE BEST prosper; losers struggle and sometimes die.

How deeply THE BEST myth pervades the world of

sports became clear at the conclusion of the 1986 World Series between the Boston Red Sox and the New York Mets. After being picked to finish fifth in their division, Boston repelled several late season challenges by competitors to earn a spot in the American league play-offs. Against the California Angels, they were one out away from being eliminated from post-season play. But the Red Sox fought back and won the league championship. Most experts predicted that Boston would lose the World Series to the New York Mets in four or five games. Instead, the American League Champions battled to find themselves one strike away from humiliating the oddsmakers before the heavily favored Mets mounted a comeback of their own and won the seventh game of the series in extra innings.

Immediately after the game, reporters and fans infected by THE BEST myth syndrome implied that Boston was a team filled with losers and chokers. To such BEST-addicts, people are winners or losers, the best or nothing at all. Gone was any memory of a long season of victory. Remembered were one or two mistakes that contributed to the loss of the final game. The BEST-pushers will not tolerate imperfection; a single flaw spells the difference between earning their admiration or their ridicule.

THE BEST myth may benefit the economy and the sports world, but it can devastate individuals. From the world of national heroes, THE BEST myth drifted into the average citizen's life. Soon people, like the marketers of electric can-openers, began to push themselves to be THE BEST. To be THE BEST requires that people establish superiority over others. In the race for the best, flaws cannot be tolerated. Each day ushers in renewed competition. And with victory as the prize, even colleagues and peers become competitors.

As a result of this competition, many began to rate themselves in all-or-nothing terms: winners/losers,

> **To such BEST-addicts, people are winners or losers, the best or nothing at all.**

Reports that stress the COST of ambition to family or friends arouse anger or, at times, indifference.

good/bad, brilliant/slow-minded, or successes/failures. Unlike can-openers, however, people who subject themselves to the THE BEST mythology experience stress, anxiety, and emotional upheavals. People are not products. Few can prove they are THE BEST at anything, and those who do believe that they have reached superiority must then defend against a fall.

America's fascination with THE BEST can be seen in their love of stories about those who become THE BEST. Rags to riches stories abound within the folklore of finances, athletics, and politics. The rich and famous, sports legends, and political wizards elicit feelings of admiration and inspiration from those who love THE BEST.

Usually biographical sketches of THE BEST center on a single dimension that highlights how an individual defeated the odds to become Number One. Reports that stress the COST of ambition to family or friends arouse anger or, at times, indifference. For example, maybe THE BEST was an unloving spouse or an uncaring parent. Maybe to reach the top, he or she mistreated friends and stepped on the dreams of others. Many respond to such suggestions by saying, "Who cares?" This question deserves an answer: Neglected children care, unhappy spouses care, and those whose lives were crushed by THE BEST's ambitions care.

The extreme thinking that accompanies THE BEST myth can be discovered in the self-inflicted formula that preys upon its disciples. The maxim made famous by Albert Ellis takes on the following Must-If-Then approach: "I must, ought, should, and have to be THE BEST at my profession (marriage, parenting, friendship, church, golf, and everything else). If I do not perform BEST, or if others do not recognize me as THE BEST, or if life circumstances do not allow me to be THE BEST, then I am nothing — a no-good, worthless failure in a lousy world."

Those who accept THE BEST mythology in their own lives usually rely on gimmicks that allow them to feel like THE BEST. Some, in effect, say, "If I can't be THE BEST, then at least I must be perfect."

To protect their image, perfectionists create a false world. Since perfection does not exist, the task of the perfectionist is to make everything APPEAR to be perfect. No one, particularly the perfectionists themselves, should become aware of their weaknesses or failures.

To appear to be perfect, those who suffer from the curse of perfectionism severely limit their world. They act only when assured of success. Challenges that offer no assurance of mastery are met with a "Yes-But" response. The Yes-But respondents hesitate in life, they fear risk-taking. "Yes, I know I should try what you suggest, but it will never work." Translated, this means, "I cannot endure any risk of failure or of seeming to be imperfect to myself or others."

By repetition of the commonplace, many perfectionists become giant frogs in self-made ponds. However, the cost to maintain a perfect appearance can be severe because perfectionists must stand in judgment before their most severe critic: themselves. Everything they do and say receives harsh reviews. If failure occurs or threatens, they transform from self-critic to self-punisher.

"I must be perfect and be accepted by others as perfect. If I screw up or falter, then I am a worthless and undeserving person." Self-punishers throw themselves into depressions and self-deprecation to atone for their failures. Some perfectionists prefer to shift the blame for failure to spouses, employers, relatives, friends, or the world in general. In such cases, others are considered uncaring, incompetent failures responsible for the breakdown in the perfectionist's appearance of infallibility.

With good reason, the faultless ones become besieged with self-doubt. To shore up areas of potential failure, they

Self-punishers throw themselves into depressions and self-deprecation to atone for their failures.

may read self-help manuals, sign up for self-improvement courses, or seek expert advice on how they should create perfect marriages, perfect sex, perfect faith, or perfect parenting. Nothing can provide such assurances. As a result, self-cursed perfectionists lash out at themselves or others to assuage the angry parasite within. Perfectionists strive to defend themselves against their own worst enemy: themselves.

Divorce strikes perfectionists particularly hard. To them it might suggest in a public way that they have failed. As a consequence, they not only must suffer from the difficult feelings normally experienced after divorce, but also they may pound themselves with self-criticism and self-abuse. On the other hand, stepfamilies quickly learn that perfectionism finds no comfortable place in a stepfamily. In blended families, complexity usually rules the day. Never are things simple or controlled enough to be perfect. Flexibility is a prerequisite for happiness.

A mother came to counseling with a ten-year-old who displayed depression, had no friends, and frequently burst into fits of anger. The exquisitely dressed mother began the session by making it clear that she sought to be THE BEST in everything. According to Mrs. Royal, her career flourished and she enjoyed many close friendships. Mrs. Royal and her husband — who could not attend the session — were sharing their fifteenth year of blissful marital harmony. Mrs. Royal explained that her courses in parenting had given her the insights needed to meet her son's misbehaviors with the healthiest of consequences. Because her lifestyle created stress, Mrs. Royal attended yoga classes twice a week. However, she was distressed because her son seemed to be unappreciative of the riches provided him by his parents. She brought Richard to counseling to be "fixed up" before his malfunctioning interfered with his school work.

After Mrs. Royal completed her presentation, I asked her son, "Richard, what is it like living in this family?"

His response: "We live in the country, and I have three dogs that I love most. So I am not really lonely. When I come home from school, Mom and Dad are still at work. That's O.K., because I watch television or play with my dogs. Usually, when they come home they like to have a drink to unwind. I know I often disturb their conversation. I try not to because it's important for them to talk. So I usually play my computer games and do my homework until supper is ready. I would like to have friends visit. But I know that to have guests is impossible because after school and weekends we are usually busy catching up on housework and yardwork. Sometimes Dad will take me fishing. But he usually likes to fish with his friends. I like my home. And I'm sorry that I upset my parents. I'll do better."

The desire to be THE BEST is an indwelling parasite that demands a cost from its host. Did Richard need to be "fixed up"? Obviously not. The family needed to change. But every attempt at intervention was countered by a maternal, "Yes, but . . ." After each suggestion, Mrs. Royal explained why any compromise on the parents' part would spell disaster for some exquisitely built castle in their self-made world. She left the sessions without the perfect solution that she demanded — one that would transform her child into a perfect son without interfering with the parents' right to be THE BEST at everything.

Parental perfectionism spares no one of its curse. Children also fall victim to parents' expectations. Sometimes a child's superiority in one area will satisfy his or her parents. However, the curse usually demands that each child become a perfectly behaved adult-child who earns exceptional grades, creates vibrant friendships, behaves beautifully and discovers an outside interest to perfect.

Some children accept the demands of their parents' perfectionism and desperately seek to satisfy them. Others crumble beneath their parents' overexpectations and become discouraged. Disheartened children search

To be the BEST at being bad is, at the least, to be the BEST.

for significance in other areas of life — some positive and some negative. Most strive for extremes in either positive or negative behavior. To be the BEST at being bad is, at the least, to be the BEST.

Like their parents, young perfectionists begin to think in black and white. People appear to be smart or dumb, successes or failures, winners or losers, and the best or worthless. Friends, enemies, and the unknown masses become competitors in every area from national tests to playground soccer games. The outcome of the competition places each person on a *fictional* ladder of superiority. Perfectionists must overcome those ranked higher on the ladder. To become the BEST, children enter the RUSH. In 24 hours, they must make the BEST grades, develop perfect friendships, and become exceptional athletes or artists. To be THE BEST one internalizes the crazy formula that Albert Ellis warns us to avoid: "I must, should, and *have to be* THE BEST or I am a miserable, worthless person."

THE BEST mythology haunts our society. Schools escalate competition among students, and clear winners and losers emerge. William Glasser, founder of Reality Therapy and Control Theory, and Erik Erikson have suggested that by the time children reach age ten, schools decide on the losers. Winners, however, must prove themselves with each new test or challenge. Every exam presents a major challenge to the perfectionists' self-worth and mythology.

Although school losers often come from disadvantaged homes and hold little chance of winning, those who strive to be THE BEST muster little sympathy for failures. "After all," perfectionists explain, "we encounter problems of our own. To be THE BEST requires struggle throughout life. Each day the demands of perfectionism must be met. So many people strive to be THE BEST that competitors cannot waste time or energy worrying about those who fell out of the race."

No child deserves the curse of a myth that forces him to strive always to be THE BEST. Neither THE BEST nor PERFECTION exists. Instead of cooperation and friendships developing, competitors view other competitors as potential enemies. Those infected by the CURSE become their own most severe judge and jailer. To strive to become THE BEST places the perfectionist on a never-ending treadmill; every new day he must attempt to be beyond criticism. To be human is simply not good enough.

**NEW AND IMPROVED BELIEF 17
DISPLAY THE COURAGE
TO BE IMPERFECT**

Alfred Adler taught his students that to live well they must display the "courage to be imperfect." Maturity and the development of talents require people to risk being only partially successful or, at times, to fail. Risk-takers accept the fact that they are not perfect and become free to expand their abilities and skills.

Why did Alfred Adler find it necessary to teach his students to have the courage to be imperfect? Because humans seem easily subjected to THE BEST mythology; perfectionists live a safe, although self-tormented existence. They narrow their world with the hope that with each included portion they can rise above criticism. Side-stepping risks, perfectionists will not move until success seems assured. Fearing their own fallibility, the BEST-seekers wish to control themselves and others.

Perfectionists' values permeate society. For example, when was the last time you heard someone admit, "Oh, I'm just an average salesman, but I'm learning the ropes," or, "I'm a fairly good parent, most of the time"? Instead, most present themselves as THE BEST at being good, or

> **When was the last time you heard someone admit, "Oh, I'm just an average salesman, but I'm learning the ropes," or, "I'm a fairly good parent, most of the time"?**

occasionally as THE BEST at being bad. Being average or mediocre finds no place in a perfectionist's life.

The press helps to spread this demand for self-perfection. Poised like snakes awaiting their prey, reporters pounce upon the slightest imperfection in the lives or conversations of public figures. Reports of small errors sell papers. Blunders alter careers. The public has grown intolerant of imperfection in politicians, ministers, and other public figures. Even local clergy must appear to be perfect or their shortcomings are broadcast through the telephone lines of parishioners. The public does not want to be served by humans, but by gods. Public figures become either heroes or goats, brilliant or buffoons, god-like or failures.

Perfectionists display no more mercy in judging their own lives. Many, for example, demand perfection in marriage and apply the "Must-If-Then" formulas to their own relationships: "I must never fight or show anger. I should always reach reasonable compromises, be completely happy, meet the needs of my spouse, and be sexually fulfilled and fulfilling at all times. If I ever fail in any way, then I have an awful marriage, and I'm an incompetent spouse. Furthermore, I'm a no-good, lousy failure in life." At times, a perfectionist demands the same flawlessness in a spouse. If the spouse fails, then the marriage becomes awful because the partner is viewed as a self-centered, no-good waste of a human.

The Goldens wanted to enjoy THE BEST of marriages. They never fought, yelled, disagreed or seemed to be distressed with one another. But after seven years of marriage, the husband announced: "I'm leaving you. I have been unhappy for several years, and I just cannot stand it any more."

Mrs. Golden was shocked. She never suspected that her husband was unhappy. Why? To have complained, fussed, or fought would have been an admission of imperfection. So the Goldens hid their feelings from themselves and others and tried to act out a perfect fiction. Their virtuoso performances cost them their marriage.

Students of Rational-Emotive Therapy suggest that the "Should-If-Then" formula needs repair. A new and improved formula reads: "I would prefer not to fight or grow angry. It would be nice if I could reach compromises and meet both my spouse's and my own needs at all times. But I will not always meet these goals. When I don't meet my goals, then I am not a worthless person. I simply made mistakes. So what? I also do many things right. In fact, I succeed more than I fail. On the whole, I'm a good spouse most of the time." Marital partners must have the courage to allow imperfection.

The curse of perfectionism also spreads to parenting. Again the "Should-If-Then" formula enjoys controls. "I should always meet every need of my child, never lose my temper, utilize perfect encouragement, never make comparisons, say all of the right things and be an exemplary role model. If I fail, in any area, at any time, then I am a total failure as a parent." Some, instead of blaming themselves, blame their spouse or the world in general for any flaws in parental performance.

Parents are humans, too. An improved formula reads: "It would be nice if I could meet my child's needs, never show anger, always be present, use perfect encouragement, never make comparisons, say all of the right things, and be a perfect role-model. But I will frequently make mistakes. When I do, I am not a worthless parent. I do more things right than I do wrong. In fact, I'm a good parent. Furthermore, I'm pleased that I have modeled the courage to be *imperfect* so that my children won't grow up with the crazy idea that they are failures when they fall short of their goals."

THE BEST parents want THE BEST for their children. It would be nice if our offspring conformed to our wills and did whatever we wanted them to do, rather than what they wished to do. But they won't. Nevertheless, some parents demand that their children be THE BEST, make exceptional grades, choose remarkable friends, and display exemplary behavior. Any lack of success on the part of their children creates feelings of failure and incompetency within the parents.

A new and improved standard might read: "It would be nice if my child never misbehaved, loved school, earned excellent grades, enjoyed lots of friends, and did well in outside activities. In addition, I would prefer that he make life-decisions that would insure his perfect happiness and success. But he has his own mind. Often he will do what he wants to do and not what I want him to do. He is responsible for his own decisions. Like me, he will encounter problems. I may not be pleased with his major life decisions, but that's O.K. His choices don't imply that I was a good-for-nothing, flop-of-a parent. After all, I raised a human, not the perfect electric can-opener."

In the future, the majority of adults may shift their values away from THE BEST mythology and its false goals of superiority and perfection. Instead, they may support more fundamental values that promote liberty, equality, cooperation, and fair play among all people. Such a change will require that adults no longer emphasize SELF-interest, SELF-striving, SELF-perfection, SELF-criticism, and SELF-punishment. Instead, adults will try to give everyone, including their family members, the opportunity to balance success and happiness with the occasional failures and disappointments inherent in living well. People are human. They need to display the COURAGE TO BE IMPERFECT.

**NEW PITFALL 17
IMPERFECTION IS A VIRTUE**

Imperfection is not the goal of life. Some people parade their imperfections before others as if they were virtues. Their list of life-problems seems as endless as their desire to talk about them. These imperfectionists seem to strive to be perfect at being imperfect. Compliments are resisted as if they were attacks. Successes are hidden like skeletons in closets.

Rather than goals in life, imperfections become byproducts of a life lived well. Those with the courage to be imperfect rebound from their setbacks and continue to develop their talents. They dwell on the positive and are not frightened by their failures.

Some people parade their imperfections before others as if they were virtues.

MYTH 18

CHILDREN SHOULD BE PAID FOR DOING CHORES

These are perilous times in which to be a child. Gone is Walt Whitman's "barefoot boy with cheeks of tan." Gone with him are those farm girls and farm boys who awoke before dawn to complete their chores. Children of the Rush replace them. Parents thrown into the modern world often suffer from motion sickness. They love their children but have little time for reflection. Often they are unsure what roles their children should play in the contemporary home. Even less certainty exists about their purpose in the world and universe.

Children of the Rush sense their parents' uncertainty about life's meaning. Eventually, for young people the tormenting question arises: Am I really needed by my family and by this society? The tripling of the teenage suicide rate, escalating drug use, increasing numbers of runaways, a growing cast of incorrigible children, and the swelling number of school problems suggest that too many of today's youth answer their question with a demonstrative: "NO, I am not needed!"

Most communities may never be like the one depicted

> **Eventually, for young people the tormenting question arises: Am I really needed by my family and by this society?**

in *To Kill a Mockingbird,* in which Atticus taught Scout and Jim to show respect for their most intolerable neighbors. But in less hurried times, adults often spent years in one community and neighbors who lived three houses away were not strangers. There were fall evenings when footballs filled the air, as children played on yards still scarred by the map of summer's baseball diamond.

On the farm, children provided essential help and accepted their work as a part of family life. Without children's help, the family business would fail. Farm children knew that they were needed. On and off of the farm, large families also needed their children's help to accomplish the tasks of running a home. Older children cared for younger children. Cooperation from each child proved essential to protect the parents' sanity, if for nothing else! These families experienced problems, but a child's need to feel needed and important rarely became an issue.

Because grandparents often lived in the same town or within a few hours' drive, they were able to play important roles in the family. The elders passed on the wisdom of their generation, willingly cared for their grandchildren, and supported their own children in their times of stress. Because grandparents were involved in the family's routine, they encouraged the maintenance of regular schedules and positive habits in their grandchildren. As an active part of the family, these elders knew that they were needed.

In times past, most families shared a religious heritage that linked them to past generations. Sundays often became a day for church attendance and family togetherness. Religion offered meaning to individuals and provided tradition for the family. Likewise, during pre-Vietnam days, faith in our country abounded without significant reservations about the nation's mission. Sports heroes inspired children, and politicians — with well-known exceptions — seemed worthy of kissing our babies.

> **On the farm a child's need to feel needed and important rarely became an issue.**

Children of the Rush find that their families often operate in spite of them rather than because of their help.

However, families in the past experienced difficult challenges, as the myths in this book suggest. Women enjoyed little freedom of choice and few opportunities for personal development. Male-dominated patriarchies limited family communications as well as the use of a variety of discipline techniques. Minorities faced severe discrimination and abuse. During economic depressions, adults struggled to feed their children. But despite all of their families' problems, most children felt needed by their families and trusted that life itself was grounded in a universal purpose. But, alas, times changed. For many, meaningfulness seems more elusive; in fact, Children of the Rush find that their families often operate in spite of them rather than because of their help.

Family farms are breaking down, couples are raising smaller families, and women have become an integral part of the work force. Mobility — from city to city or from one side of town to another — is an accepted expectation in life. In the Rush, children are both liabilities and blessings. Who will keep the children until school begins? Who will care for children between school hours and the end of the working day? How will quality time be shared when supper needs to be cooked and the television blares endlessly? What schools will help children succeed most, and how can help be found for a child's newly discovered learning disability?

When families experience major changes, children often feel left out. Initially following a divorce, children in single parent homes usually worry about whether or not they're truly loved. If divorces fare badly, they often must hear negative comments about the ones they love. And if neglected by a parent, many children believe they're unwanted.

Stepchildren also feel the Rush keenly. Travelling from one house to the next, they often lose the needed support of their friends and the security of their neighborhoods. Life so often seems to be in uproar. Where do they fit? Are they needed, they ponder.

Parents in the Rush seem reluctant to insist that their children work in the home. When children resist completing their chores, parents find it easier to complete the work themselves than to battle with their children. Because time is the most valuable commodity of "rushed" families, many parents hire outside help to complete the family work. Because so little time remains for family life, some parents feel guilty if they ask their children to work. These children grow up without helping the family and soon believe that they should be free of all demands. Children of the Rush often expect to be paid for their efforts. Therefore, these children become outsiders in their own homes — treated like yardmen and maids. Small wonder that Children of the Rush suspect that they are privileged, yet unnecessary, appendages to the home.

The concept of quality time often stumbles into the philosophical desert of the Rush. Parents who experience guilt because of their time away from home often believe that their activities with children should involve only recreation and fun. Although the enjoyment of life seems to be an essential part of healthy family life, it does not necessarily contribute to the feeling of being needed. Quality time should include occasions when children join their parents to complete household projects. Quality time should offer a balance between work and play. With such a balance children might develop what is missing most in the Rush — a sense of belonging and purpose.

The Rush often separates grandparents from the routine ebb and flow of family life. In the transition to the modern-day family, much of the wisdom of the elders seems obsolete. At their worst, some grandparents fight change by becoming overly critical of their children's parental and professional roles. In addition, distance often robs grandparents of the opportunity to provide support when their children need help. Because visits to grand-

> **Small wonder that Children of the Rush suspect that they are privileged, yet unnecessary, appendages to the home.**

Too often students avoid those courses and majors that traditionally added meaning and a love for learning to life."

parents may often be infrequent, their role within the family is diminished. During these times, grandparents work overtime to impress and be close to their grandchildren. Sugar and the privilege of late hours become easy pathways to a child's heart. But such an approach to winning the hearts of grandchildren may force parents to retrain their children after each visit. As a result, many parents become reluctant to visit grandparents, to risk that the children will be thrown off the schedule that makes life tolerable in the Rush. Ultimately, those children who are separated from their grandparents are the greatest losers.

If feeling unneeded by the family plagues many children, finding meaning in society and in the universe can prove to be a more difficult challenge. Careers once allowed workers to feel significant indefinitely, but now almost everyone can be replaced by a better trained individual or even by machines. Today, no career appears to be safe for a lifetime. To keep their jobs, many work overtime, making personal and family sacrifices. Too often parents display little love for their professions but work in order to own the things that they do love. Children entering college take note of their parents' work patterns and seek majors and courses that prepare them for financial success. As Rollo May, an outstanding existential psychologist, suggests, "How can a business major find meaning in and love for his course work in accounting? Too often students avoid those courses and majors that traditionally added meaning and a love for learning to life."

Other areas of life that once offered meaning now lie in disarray. The Sunday activities of the past frequently have been replaced by an inconsistent commitment to religion and a variety of recreational pursuits. Sunday has now become a mini-Rush and is dedicated to the enjoyment of life before the necessity of returning to Monday's blitz. It is not so much that people doubt the religious beliefs of the past as that they have lost the time and inclination to verify those truths for their own lives.

Our national mission and politics fare no better. Vietnam brought with it questions about the sacredness of the United States' goals in the world. Citizens seem to hope rather than to believe, that our country follows the right course. Elections should provide opportunities for us to assure ourselves that our path is correct. But politicians are still seen in the shadow cast by Watergate which raped people of their confidence in the political system. Even in the pastime of sports, our youth witness too many models of greed and decadence to allow a healthy love for sports to flourish. Children of the Rush look for meaning in life. They need to feel significant and needed. But are they?

Modern families must dedicate themselves to helping their children live meaningful lives. Parents need to organize the family so that children are needed, rather than becoming problematic additions to the Rush of life.

NEW AND IMPROVED BELIEF 18 CHORES HELP CHILDREN TO FEEL NEEDED

Children of the Rush must feel needed. Helping children feel a sense of importance and a faith in something beyond self-interest may pose our most difficult challenge to modern family life. True, a few families still flourish because of the work of their children. But for most modern families, a child's work is often limited to what parents can implore and often force them to accomplish. Families need to discover how to work, communicate, and play in the modern era.

In the transition between the old and new eras, no blueprint exists for successful family interaction. Free

Helping accomplish the family's work allows children to feel needed.

from the limiting myths of the past, parents can explore and experiment with strategies and techniques that may foster a sense of belonging in their children. For example, each family encounters the challenge to create plans that organize and distribute work so that each member contributes to the family. Children who are hired to complete chores soon believe that they have no duty to help the family. At best, their work becomes a favor that overindulged children bestow upon their parents. Children need duties as well as rights. Helping accomplish the family's work allows children to feel needed.

Families are complicated, sensitive organizations that need improved mechanisms for communicating, for planning, for solving difficulties, for hearing individual concerns, and for creating enjoyable plans. Fulfilling these family tasks is the first step toward giving children the desired feeling that they belong. The fast-paced, high-tech world places radical demands on today's families. Can it also offer some mechanism for meeting family challenges?

One strategy that contemporary businesses use to solve their challenges was adapted by Alfred Adler decades ago to facilitate family life: Family Meetings. Often parents groan: "But we don't have time to discuss family concerns." Precisely. Scarcity of time is the curse of the Rush. To survive the Rush many families spend regularly scheduled times together to insure that good communications and positive cooperation occur. Even the least complicated businesses hold meetings to give form to chaos. Hurried, complicated families experience similar, and often more complex, challenges.

Many families hold weekly meetings while others wait for a member of the family to request a meeting. Although every family must create its own strategy, as in other areas of family life consistency works best. Several goals are accomplished in meetings. First, chores are chosen by each family member. Following the distribution of the family work, members discuss any problems that concern them. Finally, families plan enjoyable activities for the coming week.

When should family meetings begin? Now. Couples without children can establish positive patterns of communication and cooperation through regular meetings. By solving problems on a regular basis, couples soon become Married-Marrieds, rather than drifting into the self-absorption characteristic of Unmarried-Marrieds, as we shall see later. Meetings not only keep couples from drifting apart, but they also prevent anger from building to an explosive level and prevent nagging from eroding a couple's unity. In fact, many families create a rule that prohibits nagging because all complaints — except for emergencies — must await the problem-solving portion of the family meeting to be aired. Parents with older children may wish to conduct preliminary couple-centered meetings before opening their meetings to children. Couple-meetings will allow parents to prepare and practice for family meetings.

Children under two years of age may contribute little to the family discussions, but they benefit enormously from seeing that their parents rationally discuss family challenges. What a contrast to the example so many children observe when their Rushed parents yell their way from one problem to the next or ignore problems completely. In an age with high divorce rates, adults must communicate regularly in order for their marriage to survive, as well as to provide positive models that will help their children solve problems. Young children initially enjoy joining family meetings by calling the meeting to order and then by helping plan enjoyable family outings and fun. As children grow older, they enjoy taking part in all family discussions.

No tool may prove to be more helpful to single parents than family meetings. Being a single parent is, in my opinion, the most difficult challenge in the world.

What a contrast to the example so many children observe when their Rushed parents yell their way from one problem to the next or ignore problems completely.

Time becomes precious. In a meeting an adult can make plans and discuss challenges on a regular basis. Good communications become a way of life.

Stepfamilies also seem perfectly suited for family meetings. As stepchildren move from one home to another, a meeting quickly allows them to feel needed and at home. Selecting chores allows children to contribute to the whole, which gives them a sense of belonging. Also, family meetings allow the perfect opportunity for each person to be heard and understood. The more complex family life becomes the more necessary family meetings are.

Most children love family meetings because in this situation they feel important and respected. Parents must resist the temptation to unload their complaints during the initial meetings. But once the meetings run smoothly, family problems such as non-compliance with agreements can be discussed and appropriate consequences created for future violations. Probably no area teaches children more about cooperation than discussions centered on the division of family labor.

Children in the Rush rarely appreciate how much work their parents do to support the family. As families discuss chores, children learn that they must cooperate in accomplishing the family work, or their parents will not have the time to respond to their social and recreational requests. On the next page is an example of a family meeting chart presented in my book *Parenting Without Guilt*.

One member of the family lists the jobs that need to be completed. Usually it helps to begin with an abbreviated list such as the one above. Then members alternate in choosing jobs. Some readers may think: But my child would refuse to choose any task. Fine, then parents may also refuse to choose tasks. In the example above, if my son refused to help, then I would not volunteer to take him to T-ball practice. He might respond, "But I have to

Children in the Rush rarely appreciate how much work their parents do to support the family.

	Sun.	Mon.	Tues.	Wed.	Thurs.	Fri.	Sat.
Laundry	K						
Fold & Put Away Clothes	M						
Vacuum	E, M						
Clean Tubs	P,K						
T-Ball Transportation	K						
Swimming Lesson Transportation	M						
Cut Grass	K						
Earn Money	K,M						
Feed Cats	D						
Feed Fish	P						
Take out Trash	E						

Chairman	Emily	K - Dad	
Secretary	Dad	M - Mom	
		P - Patrick	
		E - Emily	
		D - Dustin	

go to T-Ball practice." Then I could reply: "You don't have to go. But I would like to take you if I have enough time. Unfortunately, it appears that I may be too busy completing other tasks to volunteer to drive you. But if you help, then I will have the time to help you." Children soon learn that chores in the home are family chores, not parental work. To receive benefits, children must cooperate.

Should parents pay children to complete chores? Of course not. Parents receive no pay for cooking supper or driving their children to games and meetings. Likewise, children should not be paid for contributing to the family. For money, children should receive an allowance that covers their basic expenses and teaches them fiscal responsibility. Parents fare better when they do not link allowances to chores. Failure to complete chores is a problem that should be discussed during the family meeting and handled by logical consequences.

At family meetings votes can be taken to decide on family rules and preferences. Although most concerns are proper for discussions, parents should not allow discussions on personal issues that may be inappropriate concerns for children. Likewise, votes should not be cast concerning topics on which parents are unwilling to compromise. For example, most families would not take a vote to decide whether or not both parents should quit their jobs so that their children could move to Southern California.

Although family meetings usually are enjoyable, they do not always run smoothly. Children sometimes misbehave and at other times they frustrate their parents with illogical thoughts. To counter these problems families soon adapt meetings to their own styles and create rules that encourage responsible behavior. For example, some families rotate the leadership of the meetings and teach children rules of parliamentary procedure. If misbehavior requires that a member of the family leave the table, then that person will lose the right to vote and plan. Sure, meetings often become difficult and frustrating. However, frustrations encountered in meetings are far less in number and severity than those encountered by families who drift aimlessly into the future and soon become victims of the Rush. After families create their own rules and unique formats for meetings, children will enjoy the occasions. Children leave their family discussions knowing that they are a valued and contributing member of the family.

Although grandparents often live too far away to participate in family meetings, all family members can benefit from their influence. Mutual respect should govern relationships among generations. For example, parents should not anticipate that grandparents will enjoy

Although family meetings usually are enjoyable, they do not always run smoothly. Children sometimes misbehave and at other times they frustrate their parents with illogical thoughts.

tending grandchildren routinely or for long periods of time. Some elders enjoy child care; some do not. As one grandparent quipped, "We love to see them (grandchildren) come, and we love to see them go." Grandparents are not accustomed to the noise and demanding schedules of young children. In addition, older adults often require time spent by themselves; babysitting prohibits such solitude.

Conversely, grandparents should respect the schedules and special requests of parents. Parents face difficult challenges in juggling schedules and maintaining sanity during the Rush. To overindulge grandchildren or to disregard their schedules creates havoc during the days that follow visits. Grandparents should establish special relationships with their grandchildren in ways that do not disorient the normal flow of family life. When grandparents are insensitive to the family needs, grandchildren will be allowed by their parents to visit less frequently.

Grandparents can play a vital role in the modern family. Most couples who live away from their home towns receive little support and help. Couples often feel isolated. With the pressures of the Rush and the challenges of maintaining a marriage, or of being a single parent, parents need help and support. Often a weekend away from home pressures rejuvenates fatigued individuals and reduces stress between spouses. Grandparents who enjoy their grandchildren can help by being assertive in their offers of help, rather than waiting to be asked by their children. It is tragic that parents often appear to be too proud to ask for help, and grandparents are too careful not to appear to be pushy. Grandparents can make the difference between success and failure in unstable families. In healthy families, they enrich everyone's life.

Outside of family life, where do parents find meaning for their lives? No matter what the source, their children need to know. If finding meaningfulness is the major challenge of the times, then parents need to share their

Grandparents can play a vital role in the modern family.

discoveries. Whether their faith is in religion or a belief in mankind's ability to solve its own problems, children thrive on a generous dose of their parents' faith. In the Rush, adults find numerous excuses not to share and practice their beliefs: Failure to share one's faith leaves children without a sense of purpose, and possibly — as Erik Erikson suggests — without a basic sense of trust for life. No child deserves the curse of living without faith in something.

Whether future generations can derive meaning from politics, sports or our national mission is uncertain. But strong children can influence our national course and can help create a world where humans can live peacefully with one another. Children who learn to be flexible and responsible and who communicate well will be prepared to give to life, as well as to make demands of it. Family life may never return to the pace of previous decades, but with new techniques such as family meetings, families can prepare children to thrive in a complex world.

"Children should be paid for chores." NEVER. Families must organize themselves so that the work of each family member is needed and each person feels valued by the family. Completing chores adds meaning to the lives of the Children of the Rush.

NEW PITFALL 18
WORK IS A CHILD'S PLAY

A child's work displays that he is important and needed. But a child's life should not be dominated by work. Often, parents who were cheated of their own childhood do not allow their children to enjoy their young years. How often, before giving a long list of unreasonable demands, some parents say: "When I was a child, my father made me work all day. All I am asking you to do is . . ."

Children need to be children. The outstanding educator Maria Montessori once said, "A child's work is his play." Although this statement was a warning to educators, it also corrects unreasonable parental notions. To develop dreams and the initiative to realize them, children need to play. But this does not suggest that children should not work.

Balance is required between work and play. Family meetings can plan for that symmetry. Lack of balance in either direction leads children to become either the dull boys and girls that "all work and no play" promises, or else rudderless children who no longer believe that they can find a significant place in life.

MYTH 19

TELEVISION IS HAZARDOUS TO YOUR HEALTH

Years ago we invited an electronic guest called television into our homes. At first the visitor appeared to be peaceful, even helpful. Few rules seemed necessary to govern its behavior. After all, the guest offered only a handful of black and white shows that any family member might see. Furthermore, its New York parents insisted that the behavior of their young should be impeccable while in another's home. For example, at one time, the network parents refused to allow their child to show Elvis Presley's below-the-waist gyrations.

But as the Electronic Guest grew into adolescence, it increasingly began to prey on family time. Caught in transition, parents failed to create rules to control the emerging beast as a friendly, well-behaved Jeckyl turned into a sinister, demanding Hyde. Consequently, the guest of the house soon ruled the roost. Television's New York parents loosened their control and new influences began to corrupt the once innocent guest. As colors beamed, rock music blared, and sex beckoned, an endless array of programming set lusty traps for each family member's attention. Our guest no longer exerted self-control, and its landlords took few steps to restrict its behavior. As a result, the electronic visitor and its children, the many forms of computer games, now run unbridled through homes as the owners throw up their hands in despair.

Television became a family drug. Taken in small doses and under the right conditions, viewing television can benefit one's health. However, like other drugs, when it is taken in large doses and against professional advice, the drug becomes psychologically addictive and endangers the healthy growth of family members. At worst, a family will sacrifice its spirit and free time in exchange for larger quantities of the family drug.

Man has traditionally fallen victim to his pleasures. For example, sexual overindulgence disrupts marriages and lures teens into the darker shadows of life. Even substances such as sugar become potential hazards when ingested without self-control. Our economy feasts upon its consumers' overindulgence. Producers push the sale of sex, alcohol, cigarettes, sugar products, guns and other items with the knowledge that their misuse can be deadly. In self-defense, the pushers rightfully claim that they are not responsible for an individual's decision to misuse these pleasures. After declaring their innocence, they create new schemes to increase the sale of their merchandise.

Pushers will not discipline the Electronic Guest; restrictions must be made by its hosts. Although the family drug can be turned off, thrown away, or severely limited, owners in many homes feel powerless in defending themselves against their crafty visitor.

Ironically, many adults' situation in regard to television reflects their general condition in the modern world — they've fallen into the trap of their own Rush. As busy families rush to and from jobs, obligations, meetings, and pleasures, television offers babysitting for their children and a mindless transition for adults. In the Rush, parents

Television became a family drug. Taken in small doses and under the right conditions, viewing television can benefit one's health.

can accomplish work in the home quickly while their children watch television. For parents television offers a non-demanding oasis where passive participation allows them to unwind between Rushes.

Parents observe and grow angry over their children's passive addiction to the drug but adults see less clearly the passivity in themselves. In fact, it is the parents' reluctance to act that allows the Electronic Guest to dominate their homes. What parents hate in their children's lives may thrive in their own. The powerlessness that parents feel over monitoring their own appliances reflects the helplessness citizens have grown accustomed to feeling in the twentieth century. They cannot control nuclear arms, terrorism, the threat of international war, inflation, or society's ills. Television becomes one more force that rages beyond the individual's influence.

Unable to control the Electronic Guest, parents look to powers outside of their home for help. If only television executives would force televisions to behave! If only the money-makers would stop selling undesirable shows and products to gullible children! If only the government would regulate our electronic guest! We have become powerless addicts of a family drug — slaves within our own households.

Addictions inflict high costs. In the early and mid-1980's, estimates of the severity of the habit and its resultant cost surfaced. Niel Postman documented the addiction with research that revealed that between the ages of six and eleven children devote more hours to television viewing (15,000 hours) than to school attendance (13,000 hours). Recent reports suggest that television now consumes two of each child's first 18 years of life. Furthermore, students accustomed to slick, quick-paced programming find classroom teachers slow and dull by comparison. Without the lure of action and entertainment, students' attention-span decreases. For many chil-

What parents hate in their children's lives may thrive in their own.

dren, school becomes an unfortunate interruption to daily programming.

As a result of television addiction, reported the National Institute of Mental Health, young people's reading comprehension, language usage and self-generated imagination have decreased. Reports from the American Academy of Pediatricians added to the dismal account of the addiction's destructive force: They observed that after a constant injection of murders, fights, highjackings and destruction, children now accept violence as a way of life. Sympathy for those who suffer is blunted. With children's acceptance of violence comes a view that the world is a mean and scary place in which to live.

While world problems appear insoluble, complex personal problems seem to disappear with a flick of a toothbrush. Postman estimates that by the end of their teen years, young people will have viewed over one million commercials at a rate of one thousand per week. As in network programming, the message is clear: Difficult human problems enjoy simple, painless solutions. How often must children see dull, unpopular Sally Slump transformed into the ravishing, popular Sally Sharp because of a change in her toothpaste preference before they believe that the same metamorphosis awaits them in real life? Quick solutions to complex problems in marriage, friendship and work seem to be ours for the buying.

In a society that spawns divorce, television promotes the view that love springs alive and flourishes through chance meetings and insipid dialogue. Television's depiction of relationships often displays only ecstasy or tragedy; rarely represented are the daily encounters that make up most of our years. Where are those cooperative exchanges that establish whose turn it is to get up with the baby or who should wash the next load of clothes?

Children choose between the "Simpsons" model of endless conflict or the "Cosby" fantasy of eternal bliss.

Successful families experience a little of each extreme, of course, but for the most part they trudge along from day to day, enjoying life and overcoming obstacles. Life in the trenches does not appeal to television pushers, nor to their viewers. Therefore, young television addicts hallucinate about their futures as they watch hours of family interactions that prepare them for Peyton Place or Disney World but not for real family life.

Children in single parent homes and stepfamilies find even fewer positive models on television. Rarely does any weekly show display the challenges and emotions non-traditional families share. Too often specials depict the brutal side of divorce or present stepparents who would make Cinderella feel blessed. Sound, nurturing relationships in non-traditional families apparently do not create shows that sell products. Too bad, for all of us.

Other side-effects arise. Children who sit with their Electronic Guest for long periods often eat their way into obesity. After sitting passively for hours, children used to kick up their heels after school. In that era, children always seemed late in returning from the playground for supper. Now, although television watching often follows the physically inactive school hours, parents can't pry their children away from their sets and pretzel boxes to come to the family meal. Children have become less physically fit and more overweight.

Who knows who the good guys are these days? Adults no longer believe initial government reports declaring their innocence and lack of involvement in international escapades. Television shows bad cops who make shady deals, while criminals sometimes perform heroic feats. Heroes drive at exorbitant rates down crowded roads and movie macho men destroy half of a countryside to satisfy their palate for revenge. "Who's on first?" Adults no longer know — and their children never have known.

Parents grow agitated. A few, disturbed by research showing that television addiction may be most detrimen-

"Who's on first?" Adults no longer know — and their children never have known.

tal to those with higher IQs, enact temporary orders restraining television viewing. Others join with P.T.A.s or other parent movements to write critical letters to the sponsors and pushers of the Electronic Guest. But too often, adults observe their children's — and possibly their family's — addiction and do nothing to combat the electronic parasite.

Once again, this generation of parents is caught in transition between a slower society and today's Rush. Parents invited a guest into their home that grew more powerful than its owners. When controlled, the guest can be a benevolent Dr. Jeckyl. But out of control — like a Mr. Hyde — it monstrously lures, then addicts, a household to the family drug. Parents often look outside of their homes for a hero to control their overpowering visitor. Like the scared townspeople in a Clint Eastwood Western movie, parents beg outsiders to save them from their own guest. No protector arrives. Now it is time for parents to pin the sheriff's badge on their own chest and say to the Electronic Guest: "Enough is enough. If you live in our house, you must play by our rules."

NEW AND IMPROVED BELIEF 19
MAKE TELEVISION
EARN ITS KEEP

"We have met the enemy and he is us," Pogo observed. Parents must define the conditions under which the Electronic Guest can stay in their home. It is the task of adults to control potentially dangerous substances and appliances found in their domiciles. Parents find it easy to be deliberate in making rules that govern the use of alcohol and tobacco. Most experience little difficulty in limiting children's snacks or their ingestion of flavored vitamins. As the most addictive family drug, television deserves to be treated with equal concern. Parents must make rules, agree to viewing schedules, and then enforce the regulations.

A father once questioned me about one of my columns, "Family Focus," that appears in the local newspaper. The column in question discussed the ways to handle the challenge of television. The man (who towered well over six feet in height) inquired: "I don't know what to do. We set rules in our house to limit the time television can be watched. But when their time expires, my children refuse to turn off the set. What should I do?" To him my response surely appeared to be overly simplistic: "Turn it off."

Parents must take charge of all family drugs. If my inquirer's five-year-old child took alcohol from a liquor cabinet, the father would act swiftly and decisively. Television can be hazardous to a child's health and violations of its use should be treated with similar severity. Until parents understand the serious effects of overdosing on the family drug, they will remain impotent victims of their own guest.

Rules always work best when children help to make them, but when a family drug like television is involved, parents must insist on their right to limit the time and type of shows that their children watch. If children cooperate in helping to set fair rules, fine; if they don't, parents must act. For example, many families limit their children's television time to one hour or less on school days. Of course, parental decisions vary from home to home, but as in other potentially dangerous situations, children must never be allowed to dictate the family's standards.

After limitations on the amount of viewing time are set, then children should choose in ADVANCE which shows they plan to watch. By selecting their shows beforehand, children expect that the television will be turned off at designated times and are less easily victimized by the television pushers' strategies to hook them

As in other potentially dangerous situations, children must never be allowed to dictate the family's standards.

into watching an endless string of shows. At times, parents will veto a child's inappropriate choices. But it works best to allow as much freedom as possible for children to choose.

Expect abuses to occur. Children's self-control and moral development, as we have seen, are no match for the slick strategies of television producers to addict them. When violations occur in your home, meet them with logical consequences, such as the loss of television privileges for the next day.

If your family loses its battle against television addiction, then "cold turkey" remedies work well. For example, remove the television for a week. During this period of rehabilitation, you and your children can create new habits and pursue healthier interests, such as reading or exercising. Removing the television at other times can also help develop positive habits. Transition periods that mark the beginning and ending of school, for example, provide an opportunity for parents to encourage the building of positive work and play habits. Otherwise, during transition periods children often choose the easy road — taking the family drug.

As with the use of other drugs, parental modeling plays a significant role in training children. If parents want their children to display moderation and self-control, then parents must model these behaviors. Parents who over-indulge themselves in soap operas, sports events, and prime time shows will more likely have children who share their addiction.

After parents change their own negative habits, they should attack the misuse of television with the passion of a recovering alcoholic or ex-smoker. In place of television viewing, parents can help children fill their idle hours with alternative family or individual interests. Ironically, once freed of their television habit, most children prefer to participate in active pursuits. But this preference remains hidden until the addiction is broken.

Parents who overindulge themselves in soap operas, sports events, and prime time shows will more likely have children who share their addiction.

When television accentuates the use of drugs, reckless driving, sexual permissiveness or adolescent suicide, parents can respond by discussing their own values in these areas.

Once television is controlled, parents can make it work for the family. Adults need to become specialists in television programming. Many shows offer opportunities for children to learn about the world. For example, public networks offer a variety of shows ranging from an investigation of the animal kingdom to an examination of life in other countries. "Mr. Rogers Neighborhood" and "Sesame Street" carry healthy messages for children. In addition, some cable networks sponsor children's science programs such as "Mr. Wizard" and specials that explore the worlds of outer space. Occasionally the major networks offer a movie that can provide a night of family entertainment. Encourage children to choose enriching shows. On rare occasions, make exceptions to time limitations and allow television to entertain the entire family. Make the Family Guest a family tenant that must work for its keep.

Organizations such as the National Institute of Mental Health provide suggestions for additional ways that parents and teachers can use television to benefit their families. By watching television with their children, parents can compare the values presented with the family's values. For example, when television accentuates the use of drugs, reckless driving, sexual permissiveness or adolescent suicide, parents can respond by discussing their own values in these areas.

Teachers can also make television work for them. Children can learn how actors perform stunts, and then teachers can discuss the dangers of attempting such stunts at home. Elementary students quickly grasp the seductive strategies that advertisers use to entice the public to buy their products. After learning advertising principles and strategies, children enjoy writing alluring commercials to sell outrageous items such as bent nails or broken baseball bats. English teachers can examine the ludicrous plots and themes that undergird many of the prime-time television programs. In the place of such unrealistic writing, students can design realistic scenarios and create practical dialogue. With creativity and effort, parents and teachers can devise many more strategies for making television work for the benefit of children.

The Electronic Guest must not be allowed to become a harmful addictive drug on which your children overdose. Instead, the appliance should be made to work for your family's benefit. But for television to be helpful, parents must take control. Pin on the sheriff's badge, and instead of running the "bad guy" out of town, transform him into a helpful citizen.

NEW PITFALL 19-A
PARENTS CAN TOTALLY
CONTROL THEIR CHILDREN'S
TELEVISION CONSUMPTION

It always seems that one child in every neighborhood finds access to the forbidden fruits of adulthood. When I was a child, there was invariably a friend who hid his father's girlie magazines under a loose board in his garage. From time to time the neighborhood kids would gather for a peek. Our parents never knew that we had entered that forbidden world.

With the advent of television and VCRs, there may always be that neighborhood child who exposes children to prohibited programming. In addition, children may take advantage of their parents' absence to experiment with the family drug. Like taking a nip out of a bottle from the liquor cabinet, children will sneak a look at shows that are strictly off-limits. Close monitoring will reduce much of a child's illicit television watching, but children will still find ways to see undesirable shows.

Children's occasional abuses in viewing television should not change a parent's strategy. Known violations can be met with consequences; unknown transgressions cannot. Parents cannot totally control their children's use of the family drug, but they can create a home atmosphere and family rules that prohibit their addiction.

NEW PITFALL 19-B COMPUTER GAMES ARE A BETTER SUBSTITUTE

Sons of television, the computer games and similar apparatus, take over a child's life with the enthusiasm of a vampire. Parents may protest, "But it's good for their coordination" or "They're so active while playing them." Don't fool yourselves. Limit computer games just as you do television. For real physical and mental exercise, your children need to run to the playground.

MYTH 20

THE MOST IMPORTANT LOVE — PARENTAL LOVE

Is it possible for any love to be more important than parents' love for their children? After all, parental love provides the nourishment that forges positive personalities. But what allows parents to love their children in a healthy, supportive way? Marital fulfillment. Parents who meet their love needs within their marriage can pass on their love to their children freely. When marital love fails to mature — or goes awry — children often become injured by the jagged edges of their parents' unfulfilled dreams. Couples who love poorly too easily become parents who love poorly.

Moving from a childless family of two to a family of three requires monumental changes. Following the exchange of vows, couples may require two or three years to develop a cooperative, stable love. Couples must balance their personal lives and ambitions with their dreams and commitment for a family; such juggling requires time. Some legally married individuals never become psychologically married; they live together as if both were single. These Unmarried-Marrieds fail to overcome individual self-centeredness, and their ensuing marital drift provides an insecure base for expanding the family.

For most couples, whether married maturely or not, the addition of a child puts stress on their marital relationship. Surveys show that as many as 80 percent of the parents interviewed report that the birth of the first child caused a crisis in the marriage. Such reports surprise few parents. Life changes after the birth of a child. Parents feel perpetually tired, and they lose the freedom to rejuvenate themselves by coming and going freely. Many become economically strapped, and most find that non-rewarding household duties increase. Few events celebrated by society bring more challenges to adults than the birth of the first child.

Mature couples respond to the first child's birth by supporting one another and expanding their love to encompass the addition to their family. However, individuals whose union never solidified react negatively from the shock. Love for their child may be sabotaged because of an immature, unfulfilled marital love. Many unhealthy and predictable problems arise when the marriage is weak.

Many Unmarried-Marrieds initiate what Carl Whitaker, a leading family therapist, suggests may be America's most common affair: the double affair. For example, after the birth of the first child, a husband may grow discontent with the quality and/or quantity of attention that his wife gives to him. Seeking recognition elsewhere, the husband may devote increased energy and attention to his work. Soon the male's passion finds its fulfillment in his affair with his career. Days, nights, and weekends find the husband in the arms of his workplace. Often, in defense, he offers the excuse that he is building a solid financial base to support his children.

Alone both in time and spirit, the wife's passion remains unfulfilled by the marriage. Her passion requires an outlet and the child provides a secondary target. Soon

> For most couples, whether married maturely or not, the addition of a child puts stress on their marital relationship.

the mother's passion may manifest itself in an over-involvement with her child's life. Now both parents enjoy affairs that allow the immature marital love to survive despite its lack of passion. The child, who is emotionally unequipped to handle affairs, pays for the costs of this arrangement.

Shawn Peterson appeared to suffer from an attention deficit disorder. At a school official's request, his parents brought Shawn for counseling. As we met for the first time, Mrs. Peterson corrected Shawn several times before the introductions were concluded. For a four-year-old, Shawn's behavior seemed appropriate; nevertheless, each twitch from Shawn drew Mrs. Peterson's ire. During our hour together, Mr. Peterson never corrected Shawn, and Mrs. Peterson never missed the opportunity to do so.

Soon an overly familiar story unfolded. After the birth of Shawn, Mr. Peterson applied for and received a promotion. As a leading salesman in his company, Mr. Peterson earned recognition and praise from his superiors. Mr. Peterson felt less successful in his duties as a husband and father. Therefore, he devoted even more time to what he did best — business. Left alone, Mrs. Peterson directed her energies toward Shawn. Poor Shawn couldn't go to the bathroom without maternal supervision. In fact, his inadequate aim at the toilet became a frequent topic of conversation. As a result of constant criticism, Shawn became overwhelmed by his apparent lack of ability to succeed in anything. After all, when a person cannot urinate successfully, what can he do well? Hyperactivity allowed Shawn to escape from his mother's vigilance. The diagnosis of an attention deficit disorder also absolved the parents of any apparent responsibility. Shawn Peterson's "disability" provided a common interest for the Petersons and allowed them to remain Unmarried-Marrieds.

Other couples may handle their anger toward one another indirectly. Often side issues become the battle-

> Mr. Peterson felt less successful in his duties as a husband and father. Therefore, he devoted even more time to what he did best — business. Left alone, Mrs. Peterson directed her energies toward Shawn.

Sometimes Unmarried-Marrieds prop up their struggling marriage by uniting in a mock battle against their child.

ground, instead of the major concerns. For example, Mr. Merritt resented his wife's decision to return to work two years after the birth of their first child, Sandra. Her return to work appeared to fuel Mrs. Merritt's determination to spend her free time with Sandra. Mr. Merritt felt left out.

Instead of handling the problem directly, Mr. Merritt became a parental sniper; he began to sabotage his wife's efforts to discipline their child. For example, when Mrs. Merritt would request that Sandra take her bath, Mr. Merritt would respond childishly: "Oh, does she have to? Can't she stay up a little longer?" Soon Sandra ran to her father's side whenever Mrs. Merritt needed to discipline her. To Sandra, Dad seemed like a hero, and Mom became the villain. Mr. Merritt's anger disrupted the family. Everyone suffered because of indirect parental communications.

Sometimes Unmarried-Marrieds prop up their struggling marriage by uniting in a mock battle against their child. When couples fail to create a mature bond, they may believe that their children are an intrusion on their marital relationship. Often this occurs when one spouse (or both spouses) lacks the concern and love necessary to expand to a family of three. Unfortunately, parents seek unity in a contrived struggle for survival against a common enemy: their child.

Charles and Melissa Hunley married one year before Dabney entered their lives. Charles hoped to become a college professor, but the birth of Dabney prevented him from applying for doctoral programs. Mr. Hunley blamed his daughter for his situation and walked out on his family. Melissa Hunley needed Charles; she could not bear life as a single parent. Melissa begged Charles to return. After making unreasonable demands for Melissa's future time and energy, the prodigal husband returned.

Charles Hunley ignored Dabney. He never played with her or provided care. Furthermore, he became angry when Melissa spent her time with Dabney. Highly dependent, Melissa gave in to Charles' demands that she ignore Dabney. Mrs. Hunley spent less and less time with her daughter. As a result, Dabney — like a pet one cares for but does not enjoy — was well fed and watered, but not loved.

In other situations, parents attack rather than ignore their child. Mike and Tina Girvin's tempestuous relationship stormed on long before the arrival of their son, Tony. After his birth, the relationship retained its ferocity, but the blame for the disharmony shifted to Tony. "If we could only escape at night like we used to . . ." "If Tony's crying didn't leave us exhausted in the mornings . . ." "If Tony didn't catch every cold that comes to town . . ." And so the condemnations mounted.

Unofficially, the couple agreed to blame Tony for their problems. The Girvins openly united in a war against their son. As Tony grew older, his lack of positive interactions with his parents prevented him from learning the skills of basic human relations that are necessary to enhance the growth of friendships. Tony withdrew, becoming silent and angry — a child ready to explode. Whenever the Girvins' marriage floundered, Mr. Girvin increased his abusiveness toward Tony. The Girvins sacrificed Tony's life to resuscitate their marriage.

> Children sacrifice their own welfare in . . . ways that brace weak parental unions.

Children sacrifice their own welfare in other ways that brace weak parental unions. Family therapists often observe children assume psychosomatic illnesses, engage in negative behaviors, or create other emergencies that temporarily unite their parents.

The Barnett family shared few interests and little joy. Mr. and Mrs. Barnett were a couple ill-suited for marriage. Any interests either enjoyed before marriage disappeared afterwards. Their three children became their only mutual interest. Mrs. Barnett concentrated her interests on the health of her children. As if on cue, each child became ill or injured on a rotating basis. Rarely were two people incapacitated at once, but each family mem-

To visit the Barnetts was like taking a journey through the medical archives of the Mayo Clinic.

ber shared in the responsibility to provide the family with medical excitement.

To visit the Barnetts was like taking a journey through the medical archives of the Mayo clinic. Discussions revolved around exciting events such as James' most recent asthma attack, Betsy's broken wrist, or Justin's bout with pneumonia. On and on flowed the descriptions of illnesses. The family's Crisis Rotation System soon became obvious to everyone but the Barnetts. The illnesses and accidents provided the Barnett family with a shared mission. If it were not for their physical crises, what would the Barnetts have in common? What would they talk about? Their rotating problems offered a common interest, a sense of purpose (healing the present affliction), and an anticipatory excitement over future illnesses. Families such as the Barnetts could be helped, but they rarely believe that they have a problem. After all, the family that solves crises together stays together.

Some children become trouble-shooters who calm their parents' marital tensions by providing distracting side shows. Alex and Renee Moffit realized that their marriage was weak. But they yielded to the ancient myth — "stay together for the children's sake." However, these Unmarried-Marrieds openly displayed their disagreements and frequently fought in the presence of their children. The Moffitts overestimated their childrens' ability to understand marital conflict.

Troy, age nine, panicked when his parents' fighting intensified. As time passed, Troy discovered that he possessed a magic power to bring his combative parents into a peaceful alliance. Whenever Troy disrupted school or committed delinquent acts, such as shoplifting, his parents would intervene. With the common mission to save their son, the Moffitts would unite and cooperate. A family routine developed. The Unmarried-Marrieds fought; Troy created trouble; the parents united; then the cycle repeated. When they arranged counseling for Troy, a counselor exposed their routine to the Moffitts. Soon Troy abandoned his position in the family as sacrificial lamb, and the parents began the process of becoming Married-Marrieds.

When marital love proves weak, children suffer. Young people often pay a stiff price for their parents' marital problems. A parent's love for a child is essential. But enriching love between husbands and wives comes first.

NEW AND IMPROVED BELIEF 20
THE MOST IMPORTANT LOVE —
MARITAL LOVE

Children pass swiftly through the home of their parents. Couples may remain there for decades. Good marriages are not created at the altar but built in the crucial years that follow the exchange of marital promises. Creating a cooperative, caring marriage requires time and must not be rushed.

Bearing children too soon freezes the growth of a marriage. Before becoming a family of three, Unmarried-Marrieds need to spend several years completing their marriage. To move from being two single individuals to being Married-Marrieds requires the creation of joint goals, shared responsibilities, and positive communication. Couples learn to solve problems, share emotions, care for one another, and trust each other's intentions. Only after couples have become truly married can they successfully commit to becoming a family of three.

Expanding a family by 50 percent puts stress on marital bonds. As with most shocks in life, mature couples adapt while Unmarried-Marrieds begin to dysfunction.

Couples who nourish stepfamilies learn the importance of a strong marital bond, perhaps more quickly than

> **Bearing children too soon freezes the growth of a marriage.**

other married adults. A 60 percent divorce rate among couples in stepfamilies testifies to the complex challenges these couples face. Adults in stepfamilies have no time to prepare before raising children. If not together emotionally, couples can quickly be divided by their children. As in other families, no relationship proves to be more crucial in a stepfamily than the marital partners'. As the marriage goes, so goes the family.

How can Married-Marrieds continue to enrich their marriages during the demanding parenting years? Most people recite, as if by reflex, the old adage that good communication is the key to success in a relationship. But what are good communications? As Paul Watzlawick suggests, everyone communicates, even if their message is only, "I refuse to talk with you." Therefore, the important questions are: what should be communicated, how and when?

The sharing of feelings, hopes, dreams, disappointments, beliefs, frustrations and fears allows most marriages to mature. Such sharing remains equally important when a couple anticipates a child's birth. In addition, prospective parents should prepare not only for the mechanical differences that an addition to the family will make — like buying baby beds and clothes — but also for the inevitable changes in relationships and roles that will occur. Pollyanna-ish approaches that insist that changing from a family of two to a family of three makes no difference are dangerous.

Agreement over child raising issues — such as discipline — is easier to reach before the birth of the first child. Many parents who sidestep discussions about discipline before their child's birth afterwards become disgruntled by differences in philosophy and techniques of discipline. Changing ideas in mid-stream proves difficult. Parenting courses or shared study provide expectant parents with an opportunity to reach comfortable agreements and compromises concerning future strategies. In addition, taking classes such as Lamaze or those that teach other birthing strategies allow parents to positively anticipate the birth of their child.

Flexibility allows couples to adjust to unforeseen challenges that the change to a family of three brings. Never be timid about changing your plans or discussing emerging emotions. Families who adapt well can solve problems better than those who remain rigid or restrict communications.

After the birth of a child, a new challenge arises: When can couples communicate? Time becomes scarce for most couples. When exhaustion reigns during parents' early years, for example, they may go to bed at different times. When couples become too busy, an appointment or an invitation for time together becomes necessary. True, appointments rarely seem romantic, but when couples come together by schedule or accident, positive interactions can occur. Busy couples who refuse to schedule liaisons rarely see one another. As a result, the growing distance between them prevents the romantic spontaneity they seek much more than making appointments with one another would.

Busy couples who refuse to schedule liaisons rarely see one another.

To find long periods of time for togetherness usually proves frustrating. Short periods — from 15 to 30 minutes — scheduled frequently provide the consistent time together needed by parents of young children. These brief encounters provide the glue and inspiration that enrich marriages. Although to hire a baby-sitter for an evening benefits couples, many find little opportunity during these outings to share their daily feelings and thoughts.

Short, regular encounters allow many possibilities. Couples can share the events of their busy days, as well as their changing feelings and thoughts. Expressing new emotions requires little time and creates strong bonds. After the birth of a child, dreams and hopes change; adults' roles alter dramatically. These changes require that couples understand and support each other. New fears

A break from each other can render children more desirable to be near and parents more tolerable to be around.

often creep into parents' lives; after all, they live with a fragile creature, but one who should outlive them. Evenings of exchanging hopes, dreams, fears, disappointments and victories (along with concern, support and encouragement) keep marriages vital. Adding a member to the family alters an adult's feelings and stances and requires continuous communication. Married-Marrieds must not neglect the care that made their marital garden flourish.

Serious discussions need not highlight each rendezvous. Often short encounters provide an enjoyable division between one day's work and the next. Evenings can include diverse interests such as listening to classical music or enjoying a longer evening of sexual involvement. Taking turns organizing nights for each other provides a challenge that allows couples to investigate the interests of their partners. Some couples experiment with new wines and foods. Others study a favorite poet, or listen to a new record or tape.

Although the short times of sharing often contribute the most to nurturing a marriage, a change of scenery and atmosphere also contributes a change of pace needed by most couples. Outings can be for single evenings, weekends, or extended vacations.

Leaving children with a baby-sitter often benefits everyone in the family. Baby-sitters provide relief for parents who contend with autonomy-building children of preschool age. Raising children includes many periods of intensity for parents. Without relief from parenting pressures, parents easily become overinvolved. The resulting enmeshment often magnifies children's misbehaviors and conflict. Intensity in the family then swings toward negativity. A break from each other can render children more desirable to be near and parents more tolerable to be around.

Evenings out also allow parents to practice their enjoyment of common interests, as well as their appreciation of each other's company. Neglecting to spend time alone together after the birth of a child leaves individuals feeling rusty and uncomfortable as a couple. Evenings out may not be noted for brilliant dialogue or peak experiences, but outings do allow parents to focus on being together, away from the responsibilities of parenting and the home.

Weekend excursions offer rejuvenation. Time "off" is required to balance the cares of home and the stress of work with pleasureable living. Weekend expeditions allow the time parents need to unwind and celebrate life. Arranging such adventures proves challenging for couples who lack extended family nearby to provide care for the children. However, if relatives are unable to provide assistance, other couples may wish to trade baby-sitting weekends. Also college or university students may want to supplement their income by leaving campus for a weekend in the "real world" of baby-sitting.

Most adults plan for dream vacations after their children have left home or graduated from college, but many assume such vacations must await their children's departure. Parents need a dream that is closer in time. A planned trip to an old haunt or the new exploration of unseen country gives couples a goal for the future and provides memories afterwards for their evenings together. Parents who wait for their children to leave home before fulfilling their dreams may not be in a position to take advantage of their long-term plans when the time arrives.

Occasionally couples live together for years without discovering how to love each other well. Those who love poorly often become enslaved by their children and their routines. The Blanks' lives stagnated in repetition. Almost never did they use baby-sitters and when together the television served as a chaperone. The couple insisted that despite their inactivity they frequently displayed love to each other.

How did they express their love? Mr. Blanks bought

> **Occasionally couples live together for years without discovering how to love each other well.**

flowers for his wife every other Friday. On the weekends he maintained the yard and repaired their home to meet Mrs. Blanks' approval. These gifts and efforts provided absolute evidence of his love, Mr. Blanks suggested. And what did Mrs. Blanks do to display her love? She accepted and performed non-inspirational chores, such as ironing Mr. Blanks' shirts and cooking his favorite meals. These were efforts she believed Mr. Blanks appreciated.

In a marital enrichment session, the Blanks discovered that their partners wanted love to be expressed to them differently. Mrs. Blanks confessed, "It has annoyed me for years that Henry brings me flowers when he knows that I am allergic to them." Mr. Blanks appeared to be no more appreciative: "We have the money to send my shirts to the laundry. I have never understood why Judith wastes her time ironing them." The Blanks loved each other for years but expressed their love poorly.

Following a common enrichment exercise, Mr. and Mrs. Blanks each wrote a list that expressed how they wished their partner to show their love, in order of preference. Their choices surprised each other. Mrs. Blanks requested that her husband hold her at times other than when they were having sex. Also, she asked him to court her again: planning a date, arranging baby-sitting and calling her to officially request her company. Mr. Blanks asked for more time for sexual play. He requested that his wife express more interest in his career. Before this experience, the Blanks displayed good intentions but poor techniques. Once they properly communicated their preferences, they met each other's needs with more precision and excitement.

Marriage requires little work, but attention is necessary. Couples that continue to share rich times together and who express their love well will keep their marital garden free of weeds. Moving from a family of two to a family of three requires flexible attitudes and careful

Take time for your marriage; your children will become the beneficiaries.

planning. Take time for your marriage; your children will become the beneficiaries.

NEW PITFALL 20
RICH MARITAL LOVE
ASSURES FAMILY HARMONY

A good marriage provides a sound basis for family love, but it does not assure that family harmony will prevail. Good marriages evolve when adults understand one another and can meet many of the other's needs. But adults who understand and work well with each other do not necessarily understand or live well with children.

As we have seen, many couples cannot adjust to children's predictable misbehaviors, while others know few techniques for handling misbehavior positively. Others stumble into school problems or become frustrated over a child's limited thinking ability and immature morality. In short, even those who enjoy positive marriages must overcome the 21 DEADLY MYTHS OF PARENTING.

MYTH 21

WHEN THE GOING GETS TOUGH, THE TOUGH GET GOING

Family Boulders insist that others — not they — must make the changes and adjustments required by life. Meanwhile, they uncompromisingly dig in their heels and refuse to budge. Like Marines who have secured a beachhead, Family Boulders respond to all family stress with their adopted motto, "When the going gets tough, the tough get going." In other words: "If YOU must change, fine. But I will remain the same today, tomorrow, and forever."

Although the Marine motto may help soldiers during times of war, it devastates family members who struggle to maintain peace during trying family challenges. Life presents a series of predictable hurdles to families. During some of these family challenges, parents are called upon to increase their commitment to their children, and at other times they must be willing to reduce their influence.

Parents who acknowledge the changing tides of family life and who learn to swim with these challenges, prosper. On the other hand, those who ignore the changes in life's

Those who ignore the changes in life's currents may find themselves sinking into the waters of time.

currents may find themselves sinking into the waters of time. Unfortunately, Family Boulders, who lack the sensitivity and flexibility to learn to swim, usually cause one or more of their family members to sink with them.

Two challenges that require individuals to change were discussed earlier: the commitment to marriage and the addition of a child to the family. Many fail to adjust to life's challenges. For example, Unmarried-Marrieds typically will insist that their spouses change and conform to their will. Then, feeling entitled to remain unchanged, these marital Marines become uncompromising. When their Leatherneck approach fails, problems abound. On occasion, their spouses will surrender and make the personal sacrifices necessary to keep the marriage afloat. But often the cost of one-sided giving becomes too high and the marriage falters.

Some who meet the challenge of marriage successfully cannot overcome the next hurdle: adding a child to the family. In this stage of family life, parents must sacrifice many of their self-and couple-pursuits in order to provide for the needs of their children. Few, if any, "job descriptions" in the marketplace prove more challenging than that of a parent. For most parents, the stresses of raising children seem minor compared to the accompanying benefits and joys. But for others, the job leads to burn out and despair.

Mrs. Hopkins couldn't overcome the Family Challenge of adding children to her home. Each summer she sent her three children to her parents' home because the hassle of daily child-rearing became too emotionally draining without a period of respite. One day, during the school year, she called to ask if there was an agency that might house her children for a few weeks because she needed a "breather." Our conversation concluded with Mrs. Hopkins' observation: "I love being a mother, but I can't stand being a parent. Do you know what I mean?"

Every parent understands. Nevertheless, most rise to

meet the challenge of parenthood. Adults stretch themselves by developing the skills and attitudes that will allow them to meet the tests of parenting as well as to enjoy its pleasures. Unfortunately, family challenges can sometimes require individuals to give more than they are willing to or can give.

Some predictable family challenges will require that parents reduce their influence. Many who can successfully give more when asked have difficulty when required to contribute less. For example, when a child enters school, teachers assume part of the responsibility for training. Parents must ease their control. Instead of concentrating on child-raising during every moment of the day, parents now must find meaning within other areas of their lives. Many parents welcome the opportunity to concentrate on their work and other activities, but others cannot let go of their children.

Mrs. Zimmer clung to her child even during the school day. She viewed school as an enemy that threatened to disrupt her life's work of raising a family. Nothing the teachers did met with Mrs. Zimmer's approval. Soon she began showing up unannounced at the school demanding to observe her child's classes. Although her son liked his teachers, Mrs. Zimmer was critical of them.

Tommy Zimmer quickly became unpopular with his peers. They resented his mother's presence and overprotection. Whenever a teacher's behavior displeased Mrs. Zimmer, she would storm into the principal's office to complain. Both Tommy and his teachers faltered under the stress of meeting Mrs. Zimmer's expectations. Mrs. Zimmer could not adjust to the demands of losing full-time control over her child. Without this influence, her life seemed empty and purposeless. Instead of developing new interests and avenues for creating meaning in life, Mrs. Zimmer fastened to Tommy's life like a parasite attaches itself to defenseless prey. True to the Marine formula, Mrs. Zimmer dug in and became tough.

Many who can successfully give more when asked have difficulty when required to contribute less.

She became a Family Boulder. To her it seemed that everyone else should change to meet her needs while she remained the same.

Often, the next predictable family challenge involves teenagers. To raise older children successfully, parents must alter their parenting style. Parents who enjoyed exerting high control over younger children must now allow the teenager to join in creating family guidelines and plans. Most parents learn through trial and error how to work with their teenagers. They neither abandon their influence nor try to overcontrol their children. But others try to either underdirect or overdirect their teens. Their extreme approaches frequently create problems. Instead of trying to change, Family Boulders become more determined to pursue their failing techniques.

Mr. Spalding loved young children. His daughter, Marcia, was his favorite. As a youngster, she worshipped her father. Marcia followed Mr. Spalding around the house and seemed willing to do anything to gain his approval. Discipline posed few problems in those years. Marcia complied with any request or expectation of her father's. In the rare instance that Marcia became too rowdy, Mr. Spalding simply brought out his belt and Marcia scrambled back into line. The young Spalding children loved their dad, and they responded to his high directiveness with obedience.

Time passed; Marcia grew up. Her dad failed to keep pace. As a teen, Marcia developed her own ideas and beliefs and no longer accepted Mr. Spalding's point of view uncritically. Her frequent disagreements angered Mr. Spalding. What has gone wrong? he wondered. Marcia used to be so obedient and helpful. But Marcia would not back down. Soon her desire for autonomous expression found direction in an attack on the family's rules.

For every demand that Marcia made, Mr. Spalding countered with refusal. "My rules worked well in the past

To raise older children successfully, parents must alter their parenting style. Parents who enjoyed exerting high control over younger children must now allow the teenager to join in creating family guidelines and plans.

Those who refuse to bend, soon break everyone's opportunity for happiness.

and they will work equally well now," Mr. Spalding declared. Unable to influence the Family Boulder, Marcia decided to press the issue. Curfews became the chosen battleground. Marcia stayed out past her curfews in order to challenge Mr. Spalding's uncompromising control. Her father met the challenge by issuing unreasonable punishment. His message remained clear: "I am still the boss: You follow my rules or ELSE." Finally, during one fracas Mr. Spalding brandished his belt and threatened Marcia with it. In desperation, Marcia ran away from home and spent several days with a girlfriend.

Fortunately, family counseling helped Mr. Spalding adjust to the challenges that raising a teenager creates. But meeting these new family challenges proved difficult for him. Mr. Spalding preferred the old days of total control. But as his children grew older, Mr. Spalding learned that he no longer could solve the family's new problems with old solutions.

Couples in stepfamilies face problems that require wisdom and flexibility to counter. One of the first adjustments is to allow the dream of the "perfect nuclear family" to die. Adults in a new stepfamily often hope that their family-life will be ideal. Visitation, custody battles, ex-spouses, adjustment problems of children, lack of clear role expectations and a host of other challenges quickly assault the "perfect family" dream. As a result, only flexible adults succeed well. Those who refuse to bend, soon break everyone's opportunity for happiness.

Family challenges continue throughout life. When the last child leaves home, parents must adjust. Then, when a child marries, parents again must change their roles. Those who insist on maintaining old styles create family problems. For example, overinvolvement in a child's marital life is still characterized by the mother-in-law jokes that remain a common part of social humor. Some adults cannot tolerate any reduction of influence over their children's lives; instead of finding increased meaning by redirecting their energy into marriage, work, or friendships, they cling desperately to the past.

Sally Cummings complained that her mother disapproved of her methods of child-raising and constantly criticized her parental decisions. Although her mother lived 70 miles away, she seemed to know about every incident of misbehavior and all of the minor problems that her grandchildren encountered. "How does your mother know so much about your family's daily life?" I asked. "Oh, either I call her or she calls me every day. Mom can't go to sleep at night unless she knows everything that happened in my family that day." This grandmother never adjusted to the family challenge brought about by her child's decision to marry and raise children. Becoming a Family Boulder, the grandmother began to sink. In her desperation, she clutched on to her daughter with an insensitive hand. Grandmother's refusal to grow destroyed Sally's self-confidence and self-esteem.

So many people resist change. With dogged determination some dye their hair, get a face lift, and have their tummies tucked. Some alter their appearance because of personal preferences, but in other cases, their fingernails can almost be heard scratching the cobblestones of time as they are dragged against their will into the future. Life does not allow us to remain the same. In the face of family challenges, those who are flexible usually enjoy families that flourish. But Family Boulders who resist change require family members to pay a price for their stubborn resistance.

**NEW AND IMPROVED BELIEF 21
"NO! YOU CANNOT HAVE IT
THIS WAY FOREVER. CHANGE!"**

We never stop growing. As soon as we adjust to one stage, life interrupts and declares: "No! You cannot

As soon as we adjust to one stage, life interrupts and declares: "No! You cannot have it this way forever. Change."

have it this way forever. Change." Developmental theorists like Erik Erikson point to the birth process as a symbol of life's ever-changing challenge to change or stagnate. Many theorists criticize the accuracy of this traditional view of prenatal existence. However, few would dispute the philosophy suggested by the following vignette.

From the older developmental perspective, an unborn child seems to float without cares or concerns in the ideal environment of his mother's womb. All needs and desires appear to be automatically met by a caring and loving mother. Life for the unborn child seems to be calm and content—a near perfect existence. But suddenly Life declares: "No! You cannot have it this way forever. Change."

Expelled from the womb, the baby encounters the first challenge of life: "Adjust or die." Fighting to meet Life's demand, the child's first cry becomes a symbol of the will to adapt and to live. An infant displays a rugged determination to meet the first of life's challenges; his courage to adjust is a paradigm for how to handle all of life's challenges.

I heard about this paradigm as a first-year student at Princeton Seminary. At the time, I was fighting one of life's unforeseen challenges. My old ways of living no longer worked. For years I had enjoyed finding significance and meaning through athletics and academics. But now there were no more teams. And everyone around displayed an equal or superior academic ability. I stagnated, unable to return to the past and afraid to travel into the future. That was when I first heard these words of challenge from a master professor, Dr. James Loder: "No! You cannot live this way forever. Change."

Since that day I have been forced — sometimes I submitted gracefully and sometimes reluctantly — to "grow up" many times. Life cares little about our readiness to change. Time moves quickly and new challenges appear. Family members change more readily when they can anticipate the hurdles ahead. Many of life's challenges are well known, particularly those present in children's lives. Parents understand that with the arrival of each new stage their child must surrender an old way of living and adjust to a new way.

For example, to become autonomous a child must master toilet training. Until then he enjoys instant relief whenever discomfort occurs. He knows that soon Mom or Dad will venture by, feel the wetness, and provide new, dry diapers. What an easy existence.

Time passes. Once tolerant parents now issue the challenge: "Hold it!" How strange that request must seem to a child with a bursting bladder! Gone are those easy days when the child could follow his urges and Mom and Dad accept the consequences. In exchange for his sacrifice, the child enjoys increased autonomy and less dependence on his parents. Change rarely comes easily.

School days offer another well-known challenge to change or be left behind. Before school begins, children enjoy undirected and unlimited free play. When they wish to walk, they can. When they want to talk, they do. If they go to bed late, they can enjoy a nap the next day. Play rather than the rigors of homework or test preparation fills their evenings. But suddenly life says: "No! You cannot have it this way forever. Change." With help, most adjust to the demands of time.

Children, with some difficulty, begin to sit relatively still to listen to their teachers. Although resistant at times, children study and complete assignments. Their sleeping patterns soon adjust to the demands of school. Those who succeed in changing accept their new prize: a sense of industriousness and success. Those who cling to their past or lack the encouragement needed to succeed become handicapped by feelings of inferiority and failure. Feelings of inferiority will increase the problems a child may experience in the teen years.

Sometimes teenagers wish to be adults and in other moments they prefer to be children.

The period of adolescence can lead to a family struggle. Sometimes teenagers wish to be adults and in other moments they prefer to be children. Not sure of their values, many experiment and regret their discoveries. But most young people learn from their adventures and begin to dream of their futures. Maybe they will become poets who are celebrated by fellow countrymen or doctors who discover a miracle cure. Possibly they will become missionaries to a needy country, lawyers who defend the disadvantaged, or entrepreneurs who rule vast financial empires.

Soon life begins to say no to so many possibilities. Maybe their grades are not suitable for medical school or their poetry is unpopular with others. So many hopes and dreams must be abandoned as adolescents make crucial life-decisions. Finally, successful adolescents stand on their own two feet and with pride exclaim yes to a basic identity: a strong sense of who they are, where they are headed and what they bring to life.

However, some cannot forge an identity. Instead, they become lost in life's possibilities and wander aimlessly through the years. Others accept the easy road and adopt the roles and ideals of their parents. These compliant adolescents often face traumatic upheavals in their 30s when early life-decisions are reviewed with midlife intensity. As adult developmentalists suggest, when it comes to establishing identity one must struggle at some time — "Pay me now or pay me later."

Time passes. The challenge of establishing intimacy follows the struggle for identity. That the challenge to maintain intimacy can become overwhelming can be seen clearly in the contemporary divorce rate. Those unready to become Married-Marrieds cannot shift from the Me-full days of youthfulness to the We-full days of marriage. But once identity becomes secure and adults are ready to give to others, then attention can be more easily balanced among me, you, and we.

The sacrifices required to maintain intimacy can be high. One must surrender the possibility of marrying any of a host of intriguing and compatible people. Although any one of hundreds of possibilities could become a fascinating spouse, to create intimacy an adult must say no to all other possibilities. Intimacy requires that both feet be placed inside of the marital door. When people meet the challenge to create intimacy, then couples will reap the ensuing rewards for years. Humans strive their entire lifetimes to love and be loved. Some succeed early and avoid loneliness. Others continue striving to find love, or they look for meaning elsewhere.

Remember those married days before the arrival of children! How invigorating it seemed to slip out late in the evening to eat a pizza or to dance for hours. Recall those occasions when you suddenly decided to go to a movie or enjoy a party with friends. Can you recollect a spur-of-the-moment plan to take a trip, then packing in twenty minutes and traveling unencumbered for hours? Money problems were present, but most seemed conquerable. For Married-Marrieds the early years of family life offered a time to bond, a period to enjoy the thrill and challenges of living together.

The first child's birth brings with it the announcement: "No! You cannot have it this way forever. Change." Lost is the fun of sudden decisions to enjoy a movie or to go to a party. Gone are those easier financial days. No longer can the car be packed in twenty minutes. Instead, trips often require long hours of preparation and a drive that can seem endless in the company of an infant or toddler. Again, adults must adjust to life's challenges.

Most adapt. We-ness stretches to Three-ness. Children both add to and detract from a couple's life. To become a parent is not entirely pleasant. Children misbehave and for most adults, parenting does not come naturally. Therefore, parents often struggle with their tasks. Nevertheless, unlike Mrs. Hopkins who could not

> **To create intimacy an adult must say no to all other possibilities.**

adjust to a parental role, most adults adapt. Through their actions they pass on a message, "I love being a mother (father) and I accept the responsibility of being a parent." For those who meet parental challenges well, life seems worthwhile and moves forward with purpose and excitement. On the other hand, those who fail become trapped in a carousel of unhappy, repetitive days.

The preschool days pass quickly. During the formative years, parents feel needed and are, in fact, indispensable. Children's healthy growth requires that parents be dedicated and giving at all times. But soon schools welcome children and nourish their quests for a feeling of competency. If children are to succeed away from home, parents must reduce their control. They need to remain interested in their child's progress, but they must also surrender some influence to the teacher and school system. In turn, parents are challenged by life to find increased meaning from other areas in their lives. Those who cannot adjust to their limited roles often become overly involved or disengaged from their children's work. Most adults succeed in adjusting to their tasks, and their children's school years pass without trauma. However, for parents like Mrs. Zimmer, each school day becomes a challenge. Children will soon buckle under the extra weight that results from their parents' inflexibility.

Time passes. Children enter the bustling world of adolescence, and new forms of misbehaviors and new challenges occur. How simple it may now seem to parents to look back to when their children were young enough to pick up and remove from public view when the child misbehaved. If only adolescent problems could be handled so easily! But the techniques for discipline that are effective in early childhood may no longer prove effective with adolescents. A parent's role changes from one of control to one of influence. For parents who cannot make the transition, warfare or permissiveness often follows.

Mr. Spalding never held family councils and never

used logical consequences; therefore, the challenge to raise adolescents proved to be more difficult. Suddenly his arbitrary rules were no longer followed. His harsh discipline created rebellion. Clearly, life said to him: "No! You cannot have it this way forever. Change." But Mr. Spalding did not know how to change. He offered the same, tired excuses every day for remaining the same: "I have a right to control my home. I'm doing the same things my father did. I never rebelled, and my children shouldn't." Those who fight with teenagers will lose the battle. To enrich family life, parents must once again respond to life's challenges.

With family counseling to help them, the Spalding family was able to make needed adjustments. Instead of holding to his authoritarian approach, Mr. Spalding began to discuss family concerns openly. He searched for compromises with his children. Mr. Spalding discovered that teens who help establish their own rules and consequences rarely resist following them. To move away from the past took great courage on Mr. Spalding's part. Before the family ended the counseling, I heard the following exchange between Mr. Spalding and his daughter concerning weekend curfews.

"Marcia, how late do you believe you should be allowed to stay out on Saturday?" asked Mr. Spalding.

"I think 1:00 a.m. is fair," Marcia asserted.

"I'll be scared to death if you stay out until 1:00. I worry every minute that you are out late. How about 11:30?" countered Mr. Spalding

"Come on, Dad, you're treating me like a child. How about 12:00? You know that's when my friends have to be in," responded Marcia.

"O.K., we can try it. But what if you are late?" queried Dad.

"I'll call you if I have an emergency," explained Marcia.

"Thanks, that will help. But what if you are late without a satisfactory excuse?" Dad replied.

"Then, I won't go out the next weekend. O.K.?" asked Marcia.

"All right, I can live with the deal for now," agreed Dad.

The last session with the Spaldings turned into a victory celebration. Mr. Spalding and Marcia still experienced their differences, but they began to work out their problems together. In the beginning of his challenge, Mr. Spalding had resisted change, and his hesitation caused the family considerable distress. But his eventual movement created a positive family atmosphere and a renewed unity.

The last common challenges for parents occur when their children leave home, begin their own lives, and raise their own families. Their children's separation from the home further reduces their parental influence. A sense of meaning in life can no longer be found solely, or predominantly, in their interactions with their children. Parents must again grow up. Most will turn to their marital relationship, new intimacies and friendships, or their work and volunteerism to gain a renewed sense of importance and significance.

Many marriages blossom when the last child leaves home. Relieved of many of the housekeeping responsibilities and the conflicts inherent in raising teenagers, some parents enjoy an increased amount of time and energy to devote to one another. Parents shift their energies from raising children to giving to others through newly discovered or renewed interests. Those who respond positively to life's challenges remain generative and vital.

Some couples will not or cannot respond to the need for change. Panicked by their return to Two-ness, many latch on to their children's lives. Some couples never become Married-Marrieds before the birth of children. In such cases, the challenges presented by the departure of their children may seem overwhelming. In other cases, couples become rusty and no longer enjoy their Two-ness as they did in the early years of marriage. In either situation, exciting times lay ahead for those who exhibit the courage necessary to meet the challenges and opportunities life presents. But those adults who lack courage and flexibility will face stagnation and despair.

Finally, many unexpected challenges come our way, events no one wishes to experience. Illness, death, and divorce are common detours along our perfectly planned lives. Major events require major transitions. Often people clutch to the past or live lives of resentment. They fail to respond to the call to change. But for those with the courage to accept life's challenges, new worlds will open. We cannot control life's interruptions, but we can control our attitudes toward them and then make the most of our new lives.

Adults can never stop growing up. No sooner do we feel comfortable than Life says to us: "No! You cannot have it this way forever. Change."

> **We cannot control life's interruptions, but we can control our attitudes toward them.**

**PITFALL 21
EVERYTHING MUST
CHANGE IN TIME**

Everything does not change with time. Religious beliefs and family values often remain constant. In fact, it is a family's beliefs that may allow them to change gracefully as they meet life's demands. People's deepest beliefs, for example, will allow them to face tragedy and, finally, death with integrity. Our lives pass so swiftly, but our basic beliefs may pass from generation to generation.

REFERENCES AND RELATED READINGS

Adler, A. (1954). *Understanding human nature.* New York: Garden City Publishing Company.

Alder, A. (1958). *What life should mean to you.* New York: Capricorn Books.

Allers, R. (1982). *Divorce, children, and the school.* Princeton, NJ: Princeton Book Company.

Anderson, H. & Anderson, G. (1981). *Mom and dad are divorced, but I'm not: Parenting after divorce.* New York: Prentice Hall.

Dinkmeyer, D. & McKay, G. D. (1973). *Raising a responsible child.* New York: Simon & Schuster.

Dinkmeyer, D. & McKay, G. (1983). *Systematic training for effective parenting.* Circle Pines, MN: American Guidance Services.

Dinkmeyer, D. & McKay, G. (1989). *The parent handbook: Systematic training for effective parenting.* New York: Random House.

Dreikurs, R. (1968). *Psychology in the classroom.* New York: Harper and Row.

Dreikurs, R. (1972). *The challenge of child training: A parent's guide.* New York: Hawthorn Books.

Dreikurs, R. (1978). *The challenge of marriage.* New York: Hawthorn.

Dreikurs, R. & Dinkmeyer, D. (1963). *Encouraging children to learn.* New York: Prentice-Hall.

Dreikurs, R., et al. (1964). *Children: The challenge.* New York: Hawthorn.

Dreikurs, R., et al. (1971). *Maintaining sanity in the classroom.* New York: Harper and Row.

Elkind, D. (1981). *The hurried child. Growing up too fast too soon.* Reading, MA: Addison-Wesley.

Elkind, D. (1984). *All grown up & no place to go: Teenagers in crisis.* Reading, MA: Addison-Wesley.

Elkind, D. (1987). *Miseducation: Preschoolers at risk.* New York: Alfred A. Knopf.

Elkind, D. (1989). *The hurried child. Growing up too fast too soon.* Reading, MA: Addison-Wesley.

Ellis, A. (1962). *Reason and emotion in psychotherapy.* Secaucus, NJ: Lyle Stuart.

Ellis, A. (1973). *Humanistic psychotherapy: The rational emotive approach.* New York: McGraw-Hill.

Ellis, A. (1975). *How to live with a neurotic* (rev. ed.). North Hollywood, CA: Wilshire Books.

Ellis, A. (1977). *Anger — how to live with and without it.* Secaucus, NJ: Citadel Press.

Ellis, A. (1985). *Overcoming resistance: Rational-emotive therapy with different clients.* New York: Springer.

Ellis, A. (1988). *How to stubbornly refuse to make yourself miserable about anything — yes, anything!* Secaucus, NJ: Lyle Stuart.

Ellis, A., & Becker, I. (1982). *A guide to personal happiness.* North Hollywood, CA: Wilshire.

Erikson, E. (1964). *Childhood and society.* New York: Norton.

Erikson, E. (1964). *Insight and responsibility.* New York: Norton.

Erikson, E. (1975). *Life history and the historical moment.* New York: Norton.

Erikson, E. (1979). *Dimensions of a new identity.* New York: Norton.

Francke, L. (1984). *Growing up divorced.* New York: Fawcett.

Gardner, R. (1971). *The boys and girls book about divorce: With an introduction for parents.* New York: Bantam Edition.

Gesell, A., et al. (1974). *Infancy and child in the culture of today: The guidance of development in home and nursery school.* New York: Harper and Row.

Gesell, A., et al. (1977). *The child from five to ten.* New York: Harper and Row.

Glasser, William. (1969). *Schools without failure.* New York: Harper and Row.

Glasser, William. (1975). *Reality therapy.* New York: Harper and Row.

Glasser, William. (1984). *Control theory: A new explanation of how we control our lives.* New York: Harper & Row.

Glasser, William. (1986). *Control theory in the classroom.* New York: Harper & Row.

Kohlberg, L. (1964). "Development of moral character and moral ideology." In M. Hoffman and L. Hoffman (Eds.), *Review of child development research,* (pp. 383-432). New York: Russell Sage.

Kohlberg, L. (1976). "Moral stages and moralization: The cognitive-development approach." In T. Lickona (Ed.), *Moral development and behavior.* New York: Holt, Rinehart, and Winston.

Kohlberg, L. (1981). *The philosophy of moral development: Essays in moral development.* New York: Harper and Row.

Kohlberg, L. (1983). *The philosophy of moral development.* New York: Harper and Row.

Kohlberg, L. & Hewer, A. (1983). *Moral stages: A current formulation and a response to critics.* New York: Skarger.

Kvols-Riedler, B. & Kvols-Riedler, K. (1979). *Redirecting children's misbehavior.* Boulder, CO: R.D.I.C. Pub.

Krementz, J. (1984). *How it feels when parents divorce.* New York: Alfred A. Knopf.

May, R. (1974). *Love and will.* New York: Dell.

May, R. (1984). *The courage to create.* New York: Bantam.

May, R. (1989). *The art of counseling*, rev. ed. New York: Gardner Press.

Minuchin, S. (1985). *Family Kaleidoscope.* Cambridge: Harvard Press.

Minuchin, S., Rosman, B., Baker, L. (1978). *Psychosomatic families: anorexia nervosa in context.* Cambridge: Harvard Press.

Minuchin, S., Montalvo, B., et al. (1974). *Families of the slums: An exploration of their structure.* New York: Basic Books.

Montessori, M. (1964). *The Montessori method.* New York: Schocken.

Mosak, H. (1973). *Alfred Adler: His influence on psychology today.* Park Ridge, NJ: Noyes Press.

Napier, A. & Whitaker, C. (1978). *The family crucible.* New York: Bantam Books.

Piaget, J. (1965). *Moral judgment of the child.* New York: Free Press

Piaget, J. (1966). *Origins of intelligence in children.* New York: International Universities Press.

Piaget, J. (1975). *Child's conception of the world.* Totowa, NJ: Littlefield.

Piaget, J. (1983). *The child's conception of physical causality.* Denver: Arden Library.

Postman, N. (1982). *The disappearance of childhood.* New York: Delacorte.

Satir, V. (1969). *Conjoint family therapy.* Palo Alto, CA: Science and Behavior Books, Inc.

Satir, V. (1972). *Peoplemaking.* Palo Alto: Science and Behavior.

Satir, V. (1988). *New peoplemaking.* Palo Alto: Science and Behavior.

Toman, W. (1976). *Family constellation: Its effects on personality and social behavior.* New York: Springer Publishing Company.

Visher, E. & Visher, J. (1983). *How to win as a stepfamily.* Chicago: Contemporary books.

Visher, E. & Visher J. (1980). *Stepfamilies: Myths and realities.* Secaucus, N.J.: Citadel Press.

Visher, E. & Visher J. (1988). *Old loyalties and new ties: Therapeutic strategies with stepfamilies.* New York: Bruner-Mazel.

Ware, C. (1984). *Sharing parenthood after divorce.* New York: Bantam.

Watzlawick, P., Beaver, J. & Jackson, D. (1967). *Pragmatics of human communication.* New York: W.W. Norton.

West, G.K. (1986). *Parenting without guilt: The predictable and situational misbehaviors of childhood.* Springfield: Charles C. Thomas.

West, G. K. (1988). *The family: Live & in concert, selected columns.* Lynchburg, VA: The Mental Health Association.